George Orwell – Please come home. The animals have escaped the barnyard

By James F. Oshust

"All animals are equal but some animals are more equal than others" *George Orwell – "Animal Farm"* *1945*

Dedicated to all we aging dinosaurs, still populating a society that insists anything over the age of the most recent social phenomena or fad, is of no relevant value, or should be designated extinct. To those who still remember when fact and fiction were clearly understood and reality often meant surviving until the next day.

Where to Start?

To the reader, fear not. I've not forgotten the normal structure of book writing, the list of chapters and that onerous compilation of references always cluttering up so many of the last pages before the author gets to equally boring dialogue referring to all those who ostensibly performed the seemingly infinite of tasks required to get from the title to the end. Not that I didn't have the time. Or that publishers were waiting with feverish expectancy and opened checkbooks for my completion of this particular volume. Rather, I have never used chapter designations during my lifelong habit of waxing eloquently or babbling badly to friends or anyone else either required to listen or unfortunately within hearing distance of my endless verbosity. Of course I'll insert a break from time to time. Hopefully indicating a minor shift in direction or introducing another subject.

This will be how I normally talk or relate endless tales that are either of little interest to them, or more often, repetitions of past conversations in which I've forgotten previous recitations. Thus, we will wander through what is left of my memory. A journey with numerous detours and a few sudden changes in approach. Just to keep a bit of interest in exactly where I am supposedly heading. So, keep reading. You've gotten this far, so let us begin.

It bothered me at first, when setting out to pen this book; why would I waste my time compiling my thoughts and observations on incidents lost in the limited memories of today's rising millennial generation. Better yet, I could have sought to create one of those thriller mysteries, full of mad automobile chases, plenty of violence, lengthy instance of our hero's dalliances with numerous young, well-endowed beauties. An activity, which I must admit, I have no experience with during my rather quiet life. And, of course, the required literary, brutal destruction of one human life after another, for whatever noble or patriotic reason I would be expected to conjure up.

Or, how about one of those more today styled exposes in which the bare facts of equally bare human emotions and antics of the famous, the infamous, the fraudulent and those who populate the kinky world of pseudo celebrities. A true tell all work that might shock, even amuse but rarely informs or have literary value. Alas, far too many of those revelations without relevance and fiction without fact.

We could start with my ancestors and early childhood but since the first were merely names on a birth document and I had very little recollection of the second, let us move on and pursue far more interesting subjects. My insignificant beginning we can cover – briefly – later within this volume.

Now back to the reason for this particular dissertation. What has happened since the hypocritical demand that everything must be equal – except for those more equal than others?

The electorate left the barn gate open again. Now the occupants are all over the place. Corralling them has never been an easy task for the faint of heart, even more difficult when so many don't seem to care how far the animals have wandered or what they're doing.

What had we done over the past several election cycles? Thinking, when we left the gate closed, it was an expression of faith, a desire to allow the mingling of so many opinions and ideological precepts to mix freely among themselves, and that would bring compromise and solidarity. Now there's a thought that should be shelved for a few millennium. But, change is coming – or so we have been told with the supposedly surprising election of the media declared "outsider" from the mega center of liberal bias, New York City. A brash, very wealthy real estate type, called that by his many critics . . . at least the ones who don't want their true and more graphic descriptions in print or broadcasted. But sure as small puppies are like to pee on the carpet just after they're brought home from the shelter, change is surely upon us. What the future holds is not the purview of this book. I leave that up to the pantheon of pantywaist pundits and chronic worriers.

Currently we have an economy touted as ever increasing from its near disastrous fall by 2008. So why were so many people unemployed or working at positions and for hours that allows nonpayment of any benefits? An unemployment figure pronounced from our nation's capital as in the low digits. Yet simple mathematics would reveal an actual rate most likely exceeding twelve percent. But then again, who are we, the mere voters and taxpayers to ever doubt the rhythmic arithmetical gerrymandering by an administration hovering within their façade of fantasy success. Where once we were the dominant and cherished friend of many throughout the world, now, a paper dragon, expressing more fear than articulated force and purpose. We, the fabled nation of diverse participants coming together as the residue of a giant melting pot of opportunity. Today a stew of diverse ingredients, numerous among them, incompatible with any palatable offering.

With all the bellicose blathering by those with the mental acuity of a mentally challenged amoeba, the cause for the variables in stock market remain a matter of conjecture. For all those collegiate graduates in Transcendental 17th Century Literature who are still trying to figure out their duties as French fries cook at their local fast food mecca, conjecture is an axiom for guessing. I don't know when they finally realize the economy has its own syncopation, its unique beat and rhythm. First comes the boom, then the recession and inevitably the depression. In time it will reinvigorate itself and start the whole process all over again. Most governments in the world will boast they can secure their financial systems. Regrettably it is a swollen contention they are unable to support.

Alas, the newest chefs in the kitchen of social menu for the past eight years concocted a diet of suspicion and racial divide. A cacophony of harsh, damming accusations against all the traditional symbols of power and public servant cadre – police, fire and often even moving into the hallowed sanctuary of public education. But we'll leave commentary on that group of maladjusted miscreants until later. As for the future, I leave that up to the pathetic pundits of the press and moronic membership of the broadcast industry. Who knows? I don't, nor do any of you, dear readers unless this dissertation is merely fed into electronic machinations – awaiting the inevitable non-human response we expect from our computerized masters.

As this dissertation is underway we have a new force in the White House, at times a blustering and often brash individual whose resounding charge to the massive middle class that change is needed propelled an unlikely candidate into the vaunted role of Chief Executive. Although many of his stated programs and equally his demand for elimination of others was the hallmark of a surprising victory, he became the target of a vitriol by opponents and the media that has surpassed any past condemnations aimed at previous leaders of the free world. To his supporters, a demanding cry from the populace for dramatic change in what they, the self-espoused unheard class, to rid us from the almost whimsical wanderings of our benighted national governing bodies.

To his critics, gathering in crowds of, vocalizing intemperate animus, exhorting his removal, at times, by any means. What will become of his term in office – however short or full – is still for the psychics, acclaimed academic and political science tarot card readers. I for one do not have that long a tenure on this mortal earth to consider future happenings I cannot control. Nor do I more succinctly really care a damn about.

Now, on to the semantic journey I have chosen to trek. At times merely a glancing back to a time quickly passing. As the warning by the axiomatic philosopher and poet George Santayana poised, "Those who cannot remember the past are condemned to repeat it," remains ever present. Remember? Supposedly a favorite incantation of that religious freak, Jim Jones, who led all those unknowing, misguided followers to a horrific end in that stinking Guiana jungle. This particular volume is not meant to be an elegy or an archival recitation or any form historical review. Not a paean to some ideological summit nor any kind of poetical rendition since one must understand that poetry only seems to resound during war and the tremors of personal conflict. However to the historian, his or her goal is to walk through the rubble of battles that lifts their natural senses and enthuses them to declare what they have never experienced. Yet the author's pen is always at the ready, so let us clear the air before you start, dear reader.

There are so many topics resounding through the halls of academia and the less inspired hallways of our major broadcasting hubs. The newest resident of the White House, climate change or how many chunks of the Artic shelf are falling off and the emotionally charged issue of gun control and its possible effect on the long revered 2nd Amendment of the Constitution – the right to bear arms. The global terror represented by ISIS or ISLA, whatever the hell you call those bearded mental mutants striving to inflict carnage on innocent people throughout the world. Not to forget the mismatched dialogues on sexual anomalies or differences, or who gets to pee wherever and in what bathroom. We can add the health system controversy, rising geriatric population, the confused "baby boomers" and their equally misdirected millennials. Don't bother keeping count. It just continues as long as both the media and their hierarchy see fit.

But have faith, no lengthy recitation on such dreary and overworked issues at hand. We will allow all those other connoisseurs of conversational convolution to babble endlessly without substance or conclusions.

This book will cover a number of other subjects, among them, a moment or two of reminiscence and perhaps a brief trip down memory lane as it refers to those I've met and dealt with over the years. To some it might resemble the hypothetical output of a group of Neanderthals with access to a local discount computer store. A burst of contorted conversation. Hopefully some subjects may be considered newsworthy and subject to interpretation at the time of this writing. But as often is the case, such matters or controversies change in intensity or public concern as time goes on forcing the reader to recall when such recollection is not really necessary. We'll mention various champions of specific causes and those paladins of the general public, but never to extoll or demean.

Why the Weird Title?

So why pick the writer who felt his first book was of a nature to use the pseudonym George Orwell, ostensibly to spare his family any embarrassment at its's possible failure. Yet actual English author, Eric Arthur Blair, did have a fascinating life and during that somewhat brief period of literary lucidity produced not only "Animal Farm," but also the acclaimed "1984." Oddly enough, both works seem these days to reflect so much of what has happened in recent decades, or portends to seriously affect the lives of every American if what is currently progressing reaches an even direr conclusion. His heroes and protagonists may still be among us. Rarely mentioned, the tragic fact that Blair was suffering a debilitating and soon to be fatal disease while completing "1984." Did his physical travails affect his view of society as it existed then? No one truly knows so we will leave that conjecture to those more acquainted with the psyche of the author.

Orwell's renowned, 1984, presented a dystopian society that some critics of the current political controversies bears a potentially striking similarity. From that darkened view of a future world that was overshadowed by those holding the power of life and death, assimilation or rejection came the now famous expression so much in use – "doublespeak." The approved ideology in 1984, "War is peace. Freedom is slavery. Ignorance is strength," has too often entered the dialogue of tyrants and pseudo dictators over the past decades. After reading the novel itself or having later viewed the highly acclaimed movie, the paranoiac insistence that "Big brother is watching you," came to the fore by many assessing what is the true enemy of personal privacy.

Why bring mention of these literary offerings into this work? Simple dear reader. Because many of the issues I may discuss herein, certain of the present political, economic, societal and religious conditions or atmospheres that swirl through our daily existences, could easily appear related to a number of Orwell's most prolific and memorable dialogue. So we continue on this journey of recall and at times remonstrance. As Orwell wrote in "Animal Farm," "Man serves the interests of no creature except himself."

But, a brief backup. George Orwell – as I choose to use the name he is most known by when mentioning him – was accused by some as a socialist. Others debated his presumed pacifism. He went to Spain to report on the raging battles there but ended up actually fighting with the Fascists against the Communists, we are told. That is until he was wounded by a sniper's bullet and during that required period of rehabilitation, he wrote the memorable "Homage to Catalan."

Since his works always revolved around the lives and sufferings of those he considered devoid of opportunity and hope, they are imagined by many as early proof that there has always existed a sub strata of society who strive to reach beyond their oppressed state. Reading either Animal Farm or 1984, can possibly cause some serious thought as to the author's true meanings and intent. Were they precursors of what we currently experience within the Halls of Congress and the sleazy backrooms of political chicanery? Or do they just remain a part of literature in its more unique form? The decision is yours.

As a sudden news note, coming forth just as I finished this opus, China, you know, where most of the electronic gadgetry is built, has decreed the two most notable output of Orwell, `Animal Farm' and `1984', are forbidden to be read or available in that country. Possibly, reading such works would be like them looking into a mirror. Repression is the tool of the tyrant. Oppression, its inevitable product.

We Forge On

Question of the moment. Does the ability to connect lines of words or full sentences in an entertaining or instructive manner make the writer more fascinating or fashionable? Or possibly just a bit more lucid about the nature of what is occurring around him or her. Do they become more the prophet of what is real or should be? Let us end this meandering among the misconstrued – hell no!

Today our heroes so quickly disappear into the lexicon of legend and the language of occasional recall, required by historians to substantiate their research, as well as those who would doubt the appearance of the sun were it not to occur once a day. Our notables of record are often blended into a world of recollection and personal observation, yet too frequently lost to reality. They become footnotes of man's progress or decline, whichever suits the writer. It has been claimed that more books have been written about the 19th Century tyrant Napoleon Bonaparte than possibly Jesus Christ. Of course infamy and the ability to transgress and still maintain a certain celebrity status, has been the basis for sustainability throughout the Hollywood and professional sports' clique for years.

Worry not, we'll touch on more general areas and leave the specific caterwauling by left and right for future times. It is not all of my doing. Of course I will add a number of quotations, and when required by absence of provenance, some comments I've heard or read. For which there is no definitive authorship without definitive source and I will always admit are not my origin. Simply because there are many more people who have said so many more cogent and intelligent things than I could ever accomplish. So why not use their erudition?

However, those fearful of literary controversy, have no fear. I'll definitely provide the potential for disagreement and heartburn by readers who will definitely engender an opposite viewpoint. I dread the thought that everyone might happen to agree with my every opinion. Mankind does not need that type of singular direction. To peruse with social, religious, economic, legal, and of course, that potpourri of polemic perfidy – politics - I love that alliteration. However I can't, even if the reader would submit to the much expanded number of pages, include the increasing myriad of potential subjects one might even consider relevant in this compelling age of fact, fiction, fad and fantasy – too many not worth the ink. Besides, certain topics are merely brought to public attention by the winds of natural flow, never staying long enough to be worth review. Ah, and as an added subject to give cause for mental hernias or chilling the cholesterol, The undefinable subject, still so revered by the effete superficial – the world of modern or eclectic art in its most unconversant forms.

As I mentioned earlier, my approach is more conversational and definitely - not instructional - since what I have to say most likely would never change anyone's mind. It is the recognition that is found in words that create revelation – not the writer. We'll meet a subject, perhaps revisit it again and maybe a final update. Hopefully much like wandering through a milling crowd at some street festival, seeing and even conversing with others more than once. Everyone moving in the same circles without intent. The appended section titles are only to indicate where I emphasized a subject, hopefully to once more consider some additional thoughts. I will do my best to avoid hitting below the belt of reasonable proprietary – depending of course on the viewer's opinion – and my mood at the time.

Yet, let not the doubter ever believe I will obfuscate. To the younger generation, that means to bewilder or puzzle or obscurantism, much like the instruction they too often receive from their postulating pin-head teachers were they to have attended any of the liberal dogma indoctrinated dialogue produced at any college or university on the West Coast. For the eastern millennials, that would also refer to Harvard, Yale, Princeton, Columbia and other institutions of perplexity. That is unless the postulating, prepubescent student population doesn't accidentally burn their hallowed institutions down in their fury of protesting, rock throwing, convenience store ravaging and vehicle igniting. It must be recognized that the youthful mind is an untrammeled soil of potential adventure, yet to be cultivated and nurtured. If left barren, it returns to its original static nature, unable to ever produce anything of value, remaining the dormancy of the dead. If seeded with the hypocrisy of the current leftist philosophy of many major universities, it will bloom array with the useless undergrowth of inedible weeds. It is the goal of those gardeners of academic fallacy.

A Moment's Pause if You Please

As previously commented, at the time of this writing, a new president has been selected by a system utilized for over two hundred plus years. Accepted by many and dammed by those populating the losing column of electoral votes. Yet regardless of what the near future and potentially turbulent years may bring, the facts remain steadfast, the opinions proffered sit undisturbed and the purpose continues as clear as the skies above the western mountains, sans the pollution and haze that appears to secretly be man's most certain desire to blemish God's natural offerings. Let us resume the traditions of this great nation, a conglomerate of citizen input, critical outrage and the constant reminder of that greatest of personal provisos – the First Amendment of the Constitution.

Our newest occupant of 1600 Pennsylvania Avenue has become the brunt of every imaginable outrage by the assorted plethora of psychological misfits, political hacks and social miscreants – sadly, also accompanied by well-meaning citizens who have valid complaints with the new Chief Executive's rather unique if often insupportable personal comments and diatribes against critical voices. Still, those who lost the last election prize continue to undermine the global view of America with their juvenile antics and constant caterwauling. But, that is their right under a Constitution they themselves have striven over the past number of years to diminish and decry. The First Amendment gives free rein to speech and also countenances and fully protects whining, bellicose bullying and the inane mumbling of the losers in any contest – political, economic or social.

Yet, whether an avid supporter or avowed critic of the winner, when our new Chief Executive has, as the old farm axiom recites – stepped in something in the barnyard, he needs to avoid walking into the house. All past presidents have been the object of widely distributed and at times personally directed attacks submitted as humor. This current White House resident has been targeted in a manner that tends to minimize what his predecessors have endured. Yet he will likely be the continuing butt of ongoing jokes and sometimes, unproven outpourings by the sometimes emotionally challenged pseudo pundits and media for his entire term.

Where to Start – Of Course, at the beginning

First of all, I'm a citizen, born and raised in this splendorous nation. As such, granted the full benefits of the U.S. Constitution – to this date at least – unless some current administration continues to pervert the Constitutional freedoms I've enjoyed for the past eight decades. I've voted in every Presidential election since being eligible. Since my enamored, youthful advocacy of John F. Kennedy, I have each election year become more jaded and distant from tradition in my view of the cattle call of candidates being thrust at us beleaguered voters each quadrennial. That remark is not intended to disparage those who've yet to achieve that privilege. Rather, just the simple fact that I am, but one vote, among the estimated 206 million ostensibly eligible voters as recorded in 2012 national elections. Of that number, supposedly an approximate 130 million voted, an interesting 64% or so. The most current election cycle may yet reveal even greater lack of voter participation.

However, during the endless debacle of disingenuous debates and equally vitriolic presidential campaign rhetoric during the latter part of 2016, we found ourselves faced with two of the most publicly and privately disliked candidates since one comic source suggested that the Caitlin Jenner run for public office, with the imitation pop music icon, Kanye West, as Vice President. Regrettably, a mishmash of mediocre talent and incendiary journalistic encouragement presented us by both political parties, an election result where the traditional Electoral College results were overshadowed immediately by the popular vote earned by the loser. Of course it happened before. And for those on the far left, above the literacy level of an orangutan, a perusal of history refers to such an occurrence several times in the past.

Now I obtained this information off the Internet where one can find any type of weird recitals. Such as the rumored hiding of aliens from the Roswell, New Mexico, 1947 UFO crash, to sightings of Elvis by too many habitué's of the tabloid rack at their local supermarket. Even Al Jazeera, the Islamic controlled cable propaganda vehicle, jumped into the statistical fray, declaring the actual voting percentage to be a much lower 34%. Now accepting anything they say would be much like going to a nudist beach to obtain the latest fashion suggestions. Another offering of former Vice president and later elective loser, Al Gore, who added to his climate agenda earnings when he sold a heretofore little know cable channel to, Al Jazeera. As for the 2012 and most recent 2016 event, again, my vote equaled an approximate 0.0000000043 percentage, assuredly, that doesn't give me a very loud voice. But it is the voice of one individual, and dear reader, there are many, many other such individuals out there in this beautiful land of ours. Before any inferred ability on my part to be statistical whiz, I attended a major Midwestern university where the gridiron sport was prominent, and as for numeric capability, if someone called out the number three, someone else hiked the football.

I understand a major collegiate chain of schools in California wants to eliminate the expression, "America, the land of opportunity," or melting pot." Where the hell do they think the better opportunity is – some barrio in Mexico City or a tent city midway between Bagdad and Teheran, or the pollution devastated Beijing? But, then of course, we have to consider the source of such administrative asininities – the golden state of the West where sanctuary cities allow free access and protection for undocumented aliens and possible criminal elements, and where it's reported almost one quarter of the population live at or below the poverty level. The state, where in a number of the more affluent areas (spots not directly in the middle lane on the Santa Monica freeway), a house smaller than the chicken coop on my parents farm, could be listed at more than two million dollars. Of course, the realty taxes will require a salary just short of an `A-list' member of the acting profession.

My objective in authoring this volume? I would imagine we all have the right to at least one lengthy soliloquy before we finish the inevitable journey down that literary poeticized tunnel with equally authored bright light at the end. Where to begin? The political Punjabis of pomposity insist on defining various age groups with rather juvenile identification. I am supposedly part of the Silent Generation. Our parents survived the "War to End All Wars", the prematurely entitled WWI, followed by a devastating economic depression, the scarring effects of a global conflict designated World War II, soon succeeded by the chaos of Korea, Vietnam's modern valley of deaths and Iraq, Afghanistan – so reprehensibly the list continues. The "Baby Boomers" arrived. The result of the overly conception minded post WW II youth who had just left their older compatriots in the silent generation to seek the wonders of a new age and social consciousness.

They saw the rise of the intense civil rights struggle, Korea and all its lingering casualty numbers. Just as we became mired in the stinking jungles of Vietnam, up pops what some have termed generation "X´- possibly because they never truly provided and self-description. They barraged the social senses and the streets of America with endless protests. Some voicing their opposition to what many felt was an improper incursion into that particular strife. Other bull horn enhanced bellowing, at times totally without substance or reasoning and fueled in the not too distant past by the drug guru Timothy Leary and his manic mantra – "Turn on, tune in, drop out". (Flashbacks, 1963). A post teen period, creating a misunderstood wanderlust and pharmaceutical diaspora. And now the much touted millennials, promoting their self-aggrandized pillars of a new social order. An order that has dissolved into a cacophony of claimants for all they feel has been denied them. Wanting but without waiting as was the traditional process with their forebears.

My major concern, putting all these other appellations aside, is the current rising human evolution – what I have personally titled the "demanding give me" – simply, the `gimmee' generation. Today we are experiencing the soon to be in power, the vote controlling essence of youthful future political electorate. Their primary emotion . . . expectation. To be granted full adult rights, often while still pre-teens; a cost free education and subjects that won't conflict their rock music infatuation and heeding every word of ultra-liberal instructor's proclamations. To be without the risks of the real world, then off to a position. Not a job, but being ensconced with some corporation or entity that favors any educational major in diverse eastern religious dialogue or obscure psycho sciences.

Of course, at a properly enhanced wage and benefits. Those additional costs, health and income support, provided free. Critical description? I agree. Harsh? Possibly, yes. Fantasy, regrettably too true among too many of the aspiring future world changing graduates. Fortunately not all those in that age group. Yet there still exists a large part of our youthful population that appears to expect – waiting for the eventual fulfillment of their needs and desires, without the difficult trek into the adult world we all enter and must travel through. A journey to forced conformity – one style, one model, forget the accessories. Much easier to control than all those various opinions or needs or desires – or heaven forbid – free thoughts.

Simply, we are the offspring of our past and to our progeny that may exist. The most definitive hope being they will garner sufficient strength and direction in order to survive. Survival is the primary goal today in a world of constant change and varying conditions that control and allow our every activity. I've long held off writing any personal dialogue since I've never considered I had anything anyone else would ever find time or interest to briefly peruse, much less read completely. Yet, what the hell. With my time left, lessening every day, here goes.

What I've accomplished in the last three quarters of a century hopefully resulted from my basic talents and learned knowledge. My mistakes and failings merely reflected any inability and insufficiency that is part and parcel of my genetic and physical makeup. When one has lasted to an advanced age, it's far easier to admit mistakes. So many who earlier witnessed them are no longer available to further comment. As I would tell any group of youths, ever willing to listen, you attend lower school, high school and hopefully some level of collegiate education to learn needed processes. Rather basic; how to think, to reason, research, be tested, be required to respond verbally and in print. You don't become smarter at that stage. You are supposed to learn that system you will have to use for the rest of your lives. If you want to be recognized for your place in society, a society in which our parents, and their parents and all those who came before, strove to gain a place in very difficult times, earn it! To get there, to achieve any level of accomplishment, you have to learn and get smarter. And while getting smarter, which may or may not occur, you will get older and that is a proven fact. The rest is all assumption.

Written words far outlast man's ability to use them and become our most enduring monument. They can withstand the vagaries of reinterpretations by later generations and the misuse by the intellectually challenged. The principal tenet of any writing is that the opening line should reflect what the reader can expect to experience. So, this is my attempt to put forth a compendium of my personal beliefs and thoughts. Nothing more erudite – nothing more substantive than what I've come to accept as my basic beliefs. If, I, at times, seem to wax in reminiscent fashion, for any younger readers, that's what we "old folks" do. Now shall we begin?

The Present Moment

My ongoing concern has been, what if we've lost all the color in our lives? What would it be to endure unending, drab, bland, monotonous days after days? To sustain oneself during life devoid of any chromatic flourish to invigorate each future happening. Without change or variation, sadly, frustration becomes a dominant theme. Frustration's price is doubt and that is the genesis of fear. I've always looked forward to the tomorrows and those times after. Tomorrows are spiced by the condiment of the unexpected. What I fear is the institution of a fully developed entitlement society, lacking any desire to achieve which seems to me to be the intent of our present national administration.

The prevalent societal mode that disturbs me is the current emphasis on the expression "offensive" and its constant misuse. Why is seemingly every statement made in any situation is deemed offensive by some observing miscreant and then parlayed as a conversational crutch by every pseudo vocabulary reformist? To the self-imagined intellectual, they immediately excoriate anyone they determined to having crossed that indefinably invisible line between politically correct and what may have been uttered in all innocence, but immediately pronounced as being racist. Its misuse has engendered racial and political discrimination, displaying the ignorance of the uniformed and self-empowered.

We've been saying things that disagree with another's opinion or understanding of either the intent or the verbal structure of the utterance since our ancestors began putting grunts and belches into some type of less guttural syntax. As we advanced from the bush land of southern Africa to the wilderness cold and barren steppes of more northern climes, we have continued to formulate language, only to allow academic misfits to bastardize its use. From the simplest idioms developed during mankind's earliest thrusts at compatible conversation, we're now faced with being immediately criticized for any word or statement those elite of asininity have lately deigned as offensive.

Thus, the most offensive words, the most abused and arbitrarily expended expression, often without true purpose or reason, is "racial" and "racist." They are possibly the primary obscene utterances next to that four letter word referring to an attempted physical human interaction. These words are used without any intelligent thought of their impact. Their excessive and often incorrect use has become the pattern of patronizing by too many of the black leadership and the liberal inanity of the left. When expanded verbally as racial or racist it becomes the tool of either the ignorant or the wielded declaration of those seeking only self-aggrandizement. The Judas goats of the arch activists who lead the blindly devoted regardless of the facts of any situation where the expression is immediately claimed offensive.

Where did this almost obsessive preoccupation with always being fair in every decision making gesture, as they view this approach to equality. They see everything as broken, needing not repair but total reconstructing – reconfiguring – simply because they never liked the original model. To them, it is their duty, their self-indoctrinated mandate to change what they doubt or dislike – regardless the result. The current preoccupation by the maturity lacking millennials with every venue of social interaction, is a major pain to the back of the front – the butt, to be more discreet for those sensitive to the language of the average person. Politically correct groups always bring to mind body odor and flatulence. Once you enter into their particular assemblage you begin to notice the smell and then the proclivity for excessive rhetorical farting.

In the past, if offense was indicated or intimated by listeners, the primary question was to whom, why and how has had been received. Thus, voila! An apology is called for by the speaker or a diminishment of relationship occurs - or perhaps pistols at thirty feet? Here is an excellent example; a school board in Chelsea, MA, decreed that no mention should be made of Christmas in their elementary classes as such displays might "offend" atheist children. Now that's another nonsensical demonstration of the absurd. Children aren't atheist until their parents or mentors have had sufficient time to fully indoctrinate them into their own beliefs. Another school board in this great country has agreed condoms should be made available to elementary school students. I suppose for those first to fourth graders, they do make great water balloons for mischief at recess. Or do education administrators imagine a new generation of horny pre-teens? Yet, there was no outcries of it being offensive to parental purists.

Numerous liberal ideologues have decried the celebrations of Thanksgiving, Halloween, Christmas, and Hanukkah, along with various notable dates in our country's relatively short history, to Memorial Day and July 4th. Not to forget the more recently created seven day Kwanzaa, ostensibly to pacify the more activist black community. But, deny extensive coverage of the Islamic celebration of Ramadan and the outcries would be cacophonous. If we abolish all these celebratory moments in the politically correct view that they may offend one or more non participants, what then will all those new refugees, being urged upon us by the administration, have to assimilate? They will be entering into a society vacant of any particular moment of remembrance or observance. Imagine the bankrupt turkey farmers, makers of various decorations and of course – those expanses of unused Christmas trees.

Mention anything derogatory about the desert spawned religion, Islam, and Muslims are immediately offended. A fairly recent terrorist incident involving a self-espoused Jihadist in a suburban California community was supposedly sparked by the assailant's disagreement that he had to be present during an annual employee Christmas gathering. So? The door was there – better yet, do not attend at the beginning. The gay/lesbian/transgender/bisexual or per their constant insistence, the LGBT coalitions, are outraged by any hint, however indistinct or misspoke or inadvertent selection while looking for the proper word to emphasize one's personal opinion, that others just might object to their often histrionic declaration of rights. Evangelicals are displeased with other more staid religious denominations.

And God forbid – see, I can use that word – that you have the audacity to call an African American, black. Or under threat of legal retribution, the now declared infamous "N" word. If a word is offensive to your particular view of what is personally correct or appropriate or an affront to your private senses – get a life. You don't need to ignore it as having happened – you just need to move on. To continue in your own way and accept that the ignorance or unmannered nature or uncivil diatribes that so enamor some of lesser examples of the human species is their right – however degrading or regrettable their output might appear. Or often can just be considered the verbal flatulence of superficial speakers. The offensiveness of the "N" word will bring forth storms of criticism from the liberal left, the ideologically constipated ultra-right and of course the elite denizens of the Hollywood and SoHo domains. So quickly we've forgotten the constant use of that expression during the Civil Rights conflict – uttered often by the Governor of Arkansas during the Little Rock High School integration trauma. Remember him, all you righteous placard wavers? Orval Faubus. And who else came out of that same squalor of limited opportunity and denial of human rights for black Americans – your paragon of liberal virtue – the individual you heralded as the "first black president" – remember – William Jefferson Clinton.

More recently an expression has arisen from the landfill of absolutely unnecessary words like the inherent smell of rotting garbage and discarded human waste. Who cares or why is there any import if something is politically correct? We are constantly belabored by those seeking office to achieve some indistinctly acceptable standard of opinion or stated position. It has become the mantra of too many political aspirants. It has become the platform they stand on while campaigning, only when once ensconced in Congress or the White House, apparently lack the will or moral stamina to actually stand for anything that might disagree with those demanding the incumbent be politically correct.

To be politically correct is to assure that no remark or any form of expression or stated opinion doesn't vex or annoy, irritate or upset anyone else in this ever growing diverse population. I cannot understand d this almost fanatic obsession with being politically correct. Reminds me much of those small defenseless hamsters relegated to running on that constantly turning, enclosed wheel but never getting anywhere. Their young owners undoubtedly fearful that their escape from that monotony would make them prime hors d'oeuvres for one of the household's larger pets. I just have to ask, what will be the future of the English language if this battering of any expression, any voiced opinion if any use of any individual word instantly becomes both fully rejected or – heaven forbid – see I used another insensitive expression – would join the growing thesaurus of the politically incorrect. Perhaps a bland form of sign language or perhaps back to those guttural grunts and belches mentioned earlier.

Somewhere there must be an assemblage of correctness cretins who spend hours in dialogue to assure whatever is said or written has not crossed that invisible line of their dictated politically acceptable propriety. No such output is ever considered inadvertent, never a possible misspeak born out of an inability to remember all the rules of conduct demanded by the extremely leftist part of our increasingly divided society. This does seem to limit, if not totally challenges the right of free expression or the apparent Constitutional bugaboo that terrifies the liberal left and the media – "Freedom of Speech." So to those who are thin skinned in that manner or who feel this newly developed, self-endowed righteous aggrandizement is their newest mantra, beware, continually reading may cause any inner feeling of superiority to become irrevocably besmirched.

In my opinion, the true offense is the brittle nature of the insecure. Those intellectually insufficient to accept that people will say things, more often than not in haste, which the speaker may not have truly intended or understood and later regretted. This constant assault on anyone and anything that does not strictly adhere to the demanded norm, which in itself is ever changing as these self-imposed dictators of discourse continually design new barriers for others to attempt to surpass just to survive in this rising Orwellian world. These leaders of leftist lingua apparently wish to devalue man's innate desire to dream, to explore, to question what has been declared the norm. And if the occasion merits it, to be different – unlike the parade of others they might feel are in lock step to anonymity. I don't intend the need to defend every comment or belief I've enclosed herein and some reader might infer from my writings that disagrees with their distorted thinking. Just tell your equally progressivists friends to buy a copy – I can always use the extra income.

The Authorship Affliction

So, why would anyone write about all of this panoply of varying dissent and personally obsessed subjects? Just walk into any Barnes & Noble book store or other large purveyors of the written word. Look at the aisle upon aisle of books on every subject from the current political or celebrity scandal to the newest interpretation of watching paint dry. Just peruse the book section of Amazon and the increasing popularity of the "e-book" phenomena. Thousands upon thousands of volumes of every dimension, small, thin biographies of people never heard of before and whose anonymity will undoubtedly follow them to the grave. Thick, voluminous dissertations on subjects that may not even interest the author, all to become fodder for the recycling bin. Oddly enough, a number of these titles will be or are already available at your local public library; at no cost other than the human effort to visit and peruse and select that which you will be given weeks to absorb or enjoy – or both.

Many of these literary works may seem so limited in appeal, their subjects having no obvious interest to the greatest majority of the public. Yet, they keep being produced, many by recognized figures and others in the celebrity tell all vein. The newest publishing resource is the POD *or print on demand publishers* and the growing self-produced, personally financed by the authors themselves. The chance to be recognized by one's associates, and hopefully an even larger general populace, drives the spirit and eager devotion to literary attempt by so many. Now, this is not to criticize or disparage those many who desire to see their words publicly noted. Rather, we give credit to all those whose energy in such pursuits should be recognized as a desire to accomplish something of value.

So why this particular book you ask – or possibly not? Perhaps seeking a measure of catharsis? No. My past life has been of an average nature, no personal character changing tragedies, no catastrophic circumstances or abuse. No addictions other than loving the food that if favored too often, can add unwanted and difficult to remove physical girth. Drugs, only the few prescribed by my doctor when of particular need. Alcohol, limited; not that I have any aversion to its use and distribution, but because I've never truly developed a real taste – other than an occasional glass of wine or a cold beer, and only then when the circumstance or activity suggests a quaff. My illegitimacy of births is no unique situation, one experience by many others and something I had nothing to do with other than being the result of those magical sperms and equally adventuresome eggs.

Thus, no terribly engrossing past incidents in my earlier life, needing redemptive reiteration - my apologies dear reader. My intent is to voice an average citizen's view of today and to a degree, a yesterday and perhaps – just maybe - a brief glimpse at what might be just around the corner. A shouting out by one of those Orwellian barnyard inhabitants – all equal but apparently not as equal as some others.

It must be understood, if man is the only biological creature to have the capability to reason, he or she also has the greatest proclivity and millenniums of experience to be unreasonable. To all those now offended, lighten up. It's just the beginning. We have history's finest opportunity to become always cognizant of our differences. Differences that allow individualism in this country and recognition that people will differ. It is simply a concept of residing together as a society in which our forebears had proudly provided our personal freedoms with our Declaration of Independence and the U.S. Constitution. It's part of the evolution of mankind – to those alumni of Harvard or Princeton or Columbia and their western offshoots – the University of California educational system - that refers to the changing in style and nature of social conduct. See, a quick lesson and at far less cost than experienced in one of those ivy clad factories of misinformation and ideological irrationality back east.

Perhaps if Charles Darwin were to return from the theoretical beyond, and see the lack of rational evolution of certain members of the human race, he might wish to add a few chapters to his classic, "Origin of the Species". Better yet, agree he may have been in error regarding some of those similarities in the chain of human development. He would only need to wander through the chic atmosphere of Beverly Hills famed Rodeo Drive, or the frenetic club scene common in many of New York City's trendiest night spots to realize evolution is no long a slow, painstaking process but rather, more recently, huge jumps.

A Sudden Thought

I've wondered what happened to the stalwart nature of the American frontiersman we so adulated just a few decades ago. What we were taught of the indomitable spirit of the immigrants flooding our shores, seeking refuge and opportunity? That extensively diverse plethora of cultures who came to this burgeoning society as applicants for a citizenship that would require them to assimilate, to adapt, to abide by the existing rules and accept this place as their new home for generations to come. Not like today when massive numbers are either illegally entering the country, or even more criminally, being assisted by one or both of the political parties to create an ersatz voting bloc, assuring them of future election success. How did we move away from a nation of hardy, resolute defenders of personal rights and expression, to today's excessive profusion of whimpering individuals and clusters, ever vigilant to decry any comment or action by another they find offensive or in their intellectually devoid opinions, not being politically correct?

The imminent crisis of unchecked and worse yet, little vetted migrant influx, has become a major rallying point for both the supporters and the equally vehement opposition. Again, another subject I have neither the energy nor wherewithal to discuss herein. Its resolution or eventual results within our societal structure and economy will, however, remain with us for years to come. And those years I fear may seriously affect the lifespans of my children and their children – and on and on.

And so dear reader, if something herein causes you umbrage, I respect your opinion but maintain mine – but tough. That's life. You must learn life has never been, is not now or undoubtedly will ever be truly fair. Just move over to the side and let this train of commentary keep moving down the track, unhindered by the ridiculous restrictions of social correctness some will demand every remark must encompass. I read extensively and I am vitally interested in what is happening locally, nationally and globally. So there, does that make me an astute observer of all that is important? Doubtful, since there are so many issues and agendas I have little desire to explore or waste what time I have left in pursuing.

So join me, if you would, in a search to see where all our heroes have gone. Nothing presented within this volume will be spectacular or earthshaking, but hopefully a few tidbits of the unusual will emerge from time to time. There will be personal views – enough to constrict the colon of some. Undoubtedly I may trample on a few oversensitive liberal feet or those who feel it is chic to lean even more to the left, a bruised feeling or two may result.

On to the Inventory of Opinion

This is not an autobiography, save a possible kind remembrance of my own family and coterie of friends who may still remember me – however indistinctly. Most autobiographies are written by people who feel their particular life story can, in some unimaginable way, illuminate the path for the reader to see more clearly their personal trek toward the future. In this opinion impregnated soiree, I will just be an observer, a traveler along numerous paths also populated by various individuals and subjects I've met or experienced. Sometimes writers desire to clarify unknown or misunderstood aspect of their life. More often than not, to make a quick dollar or achieve greater recognition by a public on which they depend to continually bolster their own personal self-esteem. Thus, recognizing the very improbable revenue potential for this personal narrative, I will be brief to the point of sparseness on some topics, possibly broadening on others. All which I'm sure will never make any real addition to the income line on my next tax return. Still, kind of like a good laxative, makes you feel better when the objective of the dosage is accomplished.

Years ago, when faced with a problem my employer expected me to resolve, I asked an older, much wiser associate how to deal with the situation. "It's like a jigsaw puzzle," he replied. At my look of confusion, he continued. "What's the first thing you do with a jigsaw puzzle?" Without my answering, he responded. "The first thing you do is turn all the pieces face up. Only then can you begin to envision what is needed to complete the image." During my life I've tried my best to utilize this short but cogent advice when inevitable questions or quandaries presented themselves. In this book, I hope I've turned most of the pieces face up and you the reader can create the image you best feel reflects the persona of the writer or your own concept of the subjects discussed.

Lately I've begun to believe that success may be overrated, that achievement may be more satisfying to one's personal enjoyment. It gives the doer an emotional bounce that seems to last longer than the trademark signposts during a lifetime that are supposed to identify efforts as being notable – worthy of public acclaim. Achievement is often an inner admission that the undertaking was worth the effort. To me, it's a self-satisfaction that doesn't need plaudits or plaques or platitudes. Horace Mann, the lauded 19th Century educator, once wrote, "Be ashamed to die until you've accomplished something for humanity." Although not achieving that level of success, at least I hope I've done nothing to harm or disparage my fellow man – and woman; to be politically correct.

To the hip, new generational thinking, I can be viewed as an aging dinosaur, allowed to pasture in my own field of memories, of little consequence to the modern makeup of society. So be it. The youth of any critics provide them additional time on this earth, undoubtedly more attuned to whatever media output is devoted to enhancing their position within the cloistered nature of today's younger generation. A generation of newcomers who loudly proclaim that hatred is wrong. Yet continually announce to all who will listen that they hate religious people, southerners, rural people, capitalists, rich people, soldiers and more lately, police.

They suffer a new world controlled by a media and an entertainment industry determined to harvest that most prolific of produce - self-gratification. The younger of each era have, as a generational movement over the past fifty plus years, demanded a prominent position on the rostrum of public debate. Their outcries against contended injustice and disregard for the interests of the less advantaged have filled pages of print and hours of TV viewing. I appreciate and support their interest and involvement when honestly and earnestly intended. However, our youth should be cognizant of the present and look more positively to the future. They were enthusiastic supporters of the "ebony Messiah" in 2008. Interesting though, that same vociferous 18-34 age group, had the lowest voting percentage in 2012 and even les in the next election cycle. A mélange of conformists who demanded having their voice heard, sadly failing to put their vote where their mouth was on Election Day. Change comes from action, not merely shouting.

From the Top to the Bottom

In recent months I've solidified my belief that further involvement in that dusty limbo of Lebanon or stink hole of Syria and inflamed ideology of Iran, may be a bottomless abyss of futility. Wastelands of barren emptiness, controlled by equally insignificant tribal chieftains, where corruption in government and society is as ingrained as the radical Islamic Jihadist tenets of terrorism. Mankind is battling in an unseen cocoon of conflicting religious and political ideologies, firmly in place since the time of the legendary biblical patriarch Abraham. A majority of these nations in the Middle East are governed within rural, closely familial confines of tribal tradition and codes. Cultural ties forged in the heat of centuries of internecine conflict. Ties hardened by centuries of unrestrained governance and tempered by the absolute belief that to release those engrained controls is to defy both their past and their particular God. Understanding the unique quirks and centuries aged cultural intricacies of the Middle Eastern mind is much like attempting to pick up a jellyfish by the corners.

Any sane group of people might wish to consider just leaving that entire area, let the endless conflict that has raged for centuries to proceed on its own. However, removing any American or allied interests and particularly effective military presence, the result would, of course, increase slaughtering of opposing forces and especially innocent men, women and children. When they have decimated themselves to a degree that forceful resistance to any outside influence had decreased measurably, those interested observers, especially the entrepreneurial cadre, could determine if the economic and natural resources still remaining are valid reason for reentry.

However, inasmuch as America, since its conception, has held the value of human life and its accompanying personal liberty the highest of principles, such an option would never be acceptable. Thus dear reader, regardless of all the scruffy, boisterous protestors, all the anti-everything younger generation of millennials, there will be times when our country takes up arms. And unfortunately, will put certain of our military in harm's way to combat the indignities being foisted on others in the name of some idiotic ideology or equally ludicrous religious outpouring. The American people are that part of the world's populace most sensitive to the poverty, economic needs and desire by anyone to be free. Now if this intensity of care upsets or disturbs the ultra-liberal and egocentric core of today's multiplicity of dissent so popular with the media that is their right. Just a reminder, flights leaving this country are available every day.

We are engaged in mortal combat with a vicious, never ceding opponent, who survives on their hate of others. Just consider. Pakistan, ripped from a larger British controlled India in a conflict bathed in cultural and religious differences. Its eventual determination was a battlefield littered with the blood of hundreds of thousands of innocent civilians. To repeat, Afghanistan, Iraq, Iran, Syria, Libya and Lebanon are modern age rehabilitations of ancient populations, which only a century or so ago were housed in communal tent enclaves. Their people may enjoy some of our more modern conveniences today, but their distrust of others not within ancestral or religious enclosures, remains. It is this cultural crevasse I personally do not believe can be bridged for many years to come. Simple review of the most basic history of the area will immediately indicate these peoples have been warring with one another for over five millennia.

And in Africa, a number of nations, more recently dominated by Islamic thuggery', have boiled over with tyrannies that have impoverished the people and created cesspools of corruption. They join the other Islamic terrorist organizations in the denial of human rights and cessation of the most basic of freedoms – seems to be a common denominator in the lands indoctrinated by the Qur'an and the supposed mumblings of Mohammed. Mankind has been consistent in its ability to wage organized war since the earliest such conflict six thousand plus years ago. Our past has demonstrated that waging war is far better at destroying nations than nations finding sufficient strength to destroy the concept of war. Observing the many national governments and the obsequious United Nation, it gives truth to the ageless axiom, it is the old men who declare and cause war but the youth who must fight and die in those wars.

Our men and women who have, and are fighting in these conflicts, have become our greatest asset in keeping the barbarians, physically and ideologically from coming over the walls. I also believe history will eventually treat former President George W. Bush, far kinder than the malicious and vindictive vitriol spewed by most of today's media. Their misuse of the Freedom of Speech, they so long enjoyed, is merely another indication of the debasing of the ethics of journalism that has become common among current media workplaces. Did the former administration receive valid and verifiable information regarding the dreaded weapons of mass destruction, supposedly hidden by the tyrant Saddam Hussein? Who can ever be truly sure? With the nature of any intelligence gathering, accuracy is a desire and validity of information often a dream. Could the Iraqi invasion been avoided were it found no such weaponry existed? I don't know – do you? And if you did, why the hell aren't you in the White House instead of the person now there further exacerbating the situation in the Middle East? Insufficient intelligence gathering and ineffective understanding has caused more sudden conflicts than all the planned assaults in the world's history of war.

Here's a Personality Perspective

I don't dislike Barack Hussein Obama, per se. But early on, I came to distrust him. And from distrust often arises a dislike. My principal emotional response resided only that I considered him to be one of the more dangerous threats to the support of the Constitution to have ever occupied in the White House – nothing personal. Other than that, I'm sure he may have some good qualities but I leave any adulation to his adoring if not benighted fans and of course the major TV networks and the New York Times. My problem is I had come to doubt many or his declarations and administrative actions – as did many people. His receipt of the Nobel Peace Prize, awarded less than nine months after his inauguration, was an embarrassment to his constituents, a disparagement of the intent of the prize itself, and a blatant insult to those who deservedly received this monumental award in the past. Yet, that same group also gave vapid, former Vice president, Al Gore, the same award for his leadership of the emerging climate change debacle. A vaunted recognition when he had lent only his heretofore little recognized name to a campaign, actually driven and resulting in the hard work of a myriad of nameless and unheralded others.

However, it must be recognized, the members of the group determining the Nobel nominees are known dedicated leftists and socialist oriented elitists. Individuals representing groups' long proponents of greater government control on the political, social and economic welfare of the people. So Orwellian – wouldn't you say? It was interesting the nomination of potential contenders was gathered months before, a definite conundrum, but one never investigated by the media – the self-endowed proponents of always revealing the truth – and only the truth. Who nominated him? When and on what basis? What specific achievement merited his selection? Questions never publicly asked or answered. Or was it just to thumb the effete nose at Obama's predecessor.

Barack Obama should have refused the Nobel Prize, admitting he'd done nothing to date to warrant its consideration. Then he could have expressed appreciation for the proffered honor and asking that a more deserving individual be selected. Would not the public acclaim here have been enormous? His rating would have soared. But, his ego and feeling of irrefutable correctness in all matters, was too great to allow such a rational act. That self-enchantment, that evident narcissism is his Achilles heel.

One ageless truism is that you are often viewed in respect to your associates, and this was one of Obama's initial and most glaring millstones that remained around his political neck for his entire tenure. He surrounded himself with individuals, who themselves appear at times to lack even a modicum of ethical or trustworthy personas. Thus, after a lengthy period of distrust arises an eventual dislike. Eventually this becomes a complete refusal to accept the speaker's words, however sincerely intended. I find it difficult to equate his ability to be aware of the need for respected and ethically pronounced associates, considering some of his initial appointees had themselves checkered backgrounds, some with marked communist leanings and a number were of the Islamic persuasion, far in excess of any earlier administration.

For all his educational background and his meteoric rise to national prominence, Barack Hussein Obama may remain haunted and tarnished by the ever present scent of turpitude that has been the hallmark of the Chicago and Illinois political structure where he flourished. Or could it be the result of the education he received in the bosom of indulgent progressive thought and instruction, so marked within the Harvard, Columbia, Princeton and Yale curriculums. The controversy, generated by some groups regarding his actual birth location and eligibility to be president, will always be a footnote for years to come. Proven it was without any merit, his refusal to produce the much requested documentation, was merely a mirror of his constant appearance of subterfuge and lack of cooperative disclosure. His proven birth as an American citizen is without doubt. His entry to various educational institutions, supposedly as a "foreign student" will continually stain his biography, however irrelevant.

The question of eligibility for the presidency has become another of the media mandated conversations. George Romney, himself a candidate in an earlier national campaign, was born in Mexico to American parents. Former candidate Senator John McCain, himself also born outside the country, on a military base to American parents. And most lately, another recent presidential primary candidate's birth in Canada was also grist for the grinders of an overly excitable media and opponents. To this writer, our past presidents have made mistakes, and too often chosen ill prepared and often excessively biased advisors. Their tendency to find proper, equally unprepared Cabinet members and principal staff assures they must share the bulk of the burden for decisions that led us deeper into that miasma in the Middle East.

A newly created plethora of appointed "czars" by the president during the early years of his first term, were positioned to oversee numerous mandated decision making functions by traditional departments, positions, who we were told strangely enough, were answerable only to the President. Their appointments bypassed Congressional oversight and subservience, which violated the U.S. Constitution in a manner not known since WW II. The most recent past White House administration roster strongly resembled a Harvard alumni directory. But then to survive within the infamous Washington 'Beltway', one must acquire a modicum of power. That is the accelerant for success, an acquisition that signals rise to prominence for those desiring escape from their personal anonymity. Yet secret power is the only kind of power that exists whereas the public displays of power are merely sophomoric reflections of amateurs. Power used effectively is to exert its result without ever revealing the source or full extent of tis potential.

During his campaign, Barack Obama was rarely criticized in any form, by only a few media outlets, for his two decades adherence to the preaching of the rabble rousing, and obscenity prone anti America blowhard, Rev. Jeremiah Wright. A man of the cloth who the former president stated had been his spiritual mentor for years. A person of some influence, however misdirected, who reportedly spent several years in the U.S. Marine Corps when younger, apparently forgetting or disregarding the high standards of that famous corps of American heroes who wore the vaunted globe and anchor. William F. Buckley, Jr., noted conservative political intellectual, put it so well when he once wrote, "I would rather be governed by the first three hundred names in the Boston phone book than the entire faculty at Harvard."

We Must Move On

Enough for the moment about this former junior Senator from Illinois whose absentee record from Senate vote calls would eclipse the legislative action of a dead member of that body. We can speak of him later after more substantive matters are discussed. His Vice President, considered a jovial and more lovable personality, was himself a very expert manipulator of Congressional games playing, and his affable nature should not be excuse for his true political skills.

Prior to the surprising revelatory 2016 national election results, one party had literally anointed a former "First Lady", ersatz Senator and inadequate Secretary of State as its next nominee. Across the proverbial Congressional aisle, the Republicans produced more potential presidential candidates than homeless applicants at a soup kitchen on a freezing winter's night. We left their eventual winnowing out to the almost juvenile fascination with the caucus system and the media hyped primaries in states who's total population are a mere blip on any population map. Voila! From out of the forest of indistinguishable and leafless inhabitants rose a mighty sequoia – at least in the minds of the many who gave the outsider, Donald J. Trump, a victory beyond the most exaggerated imagination of any of the current self-appointed savants of the ultra-leftist domain.

In this writer's opinion, it is not how much one knows about all the complex situations facing our country. Rather, it requires someone with the ethical strength and ability to select those whose individual expertise can best assist him or her in dealing with the maelstrom that has and will continually buffet the office of the President. Will the winner of the 2016 quadrennial political quagmire will be sufficient- who knows – not I. Tune in for the future - film at eleven.

The Democrat's heir apparent to the highest post in the nation, possibly in the world, Hillary Rodham Clinton, faced off against brash, often excessively verbose in unacceptable manner, multi-millionaire Donald Trump, vociferous, loud, at times blatantly anti something or the other. Condemned by the left as racist, homophobic, anti-Latino and the female gender's worst enemy, he is adored by many in what is termed by the more liberal element, the middle class, uninformed, "white trash." Loquacious to an accelerated degree, bombastic in retorts to his critics, he still represented to many millions of potential voters determined to see changes in the Washington establishment and halls of Congress their last hope to retrieve their personal tight to have a voice in the process of government. Could better, more balanced, more constituent allied candidates been effectively winnowed from the many potential figures available? Definitely. But within the mechanism of both major political parties lay rusting gears and often inoperable parts of the machinery to make it function as hopefully designed.

The Democratic Party machine, the far left, funded by Hungarian, Cro-Magnon expatriate George Soros, the butt bussing media and Hillary's lackadaisical attitude in how to campaign to all eligible voters, caused the election result. They, in fact, created and bolstered the winners eventual surprise victory. They only need to look in a mirror to determine who is or was at fault for their shocking loss. In a foolishly inane literary dialogue, titled "What Happened", Hillary Rodham Clinton blamed an assortment of impossible sources that she has turned her post-election loss diatribes into embarrassingly ludicrous whining. It is a volume, stuffed with more misdirected accusations than an overladen Thanksgiving turkey. First it was the crooked campaign tactics of the winner, then the KKK influenced and earlier described "deplorables" she pronounced so succinctly. Soon it became the Russians, then Republican operatives, then members of her own incompetent cadre, afterwards the Democratic leadership itself and more lately it was the social media Facebook and Twitter. She has run out of those to blame – except herself.

Had Hillary Clinton become President, the first female to reach that high plateau, she would have brought with her a train load of baggage – both political and personal. Most noticeable would have been her husband, former President William Jefferson Clinton, whose escapades and often past arcane actions and private dealings has and will continue to be fodder for books, documentaries, tabloids and of course legal briefs. But now that November 8, 2016 has passed, those are matters that must be left to Mrs. Clinton to personally deal with. Accompanying her would undoubtedly have been an ensemble of incompetents, social and ideological sycophants, very similar to the motley crew that has populated inside the Washington Beltway for the past eight years.

And that is why my complaint centers on this apparent pseudo-intellectual charade affected by too many cultural and political wannabes. My adopted father came to America from then Austria-Hungary, later formed as Czechoslovakia after the end of WW I - "The War to End All Wars", as loudly proclaimed at that time. However, even with a limited formal education, he learned to speak English, a noticeable accent, but distinct enough for his many associates and friends in an Ohio farm community and the local steel mill where he worked for almost 25-years. He strove to assure he was reasonably able to be understood. He, as did so many other immigrants at the time, knew that a reasonable proficiency in his new homeland's language and culture was critical to succeeding in any endeavor. Thus he and his compatriots studied and went to classes for several years. And as an important aside, his employer paid for the classes – sessions designed to aid in the needed assimilation to a new and strange culture by all the newcomers. He would often ask me, at that time, I, a ten or eleven year old boy, if he'd pronounced an unfamiliar word correctly. He always desired to be a "good American." But more about he and my early years later, if you will be so patient to read on until then.

As mentioned earlier, today, the lengthy process to acquire citizenship has been set aside for the many flooding our borders. A shame as there are so many valuable things one should learn when making our country their home and seeking a new life. With the proliferating Hispanic population, retailers need have at least a few clerks fluent in that tongue, and rightfully so as this growing population is an increasing retail revenue source. They are told this progressive attitude will equalize the consumer's advantage in an ability to become more adapted to the American culture. I agree. Those with a limited knowledge of our common language should be afforded assistance. However, where is the emphasis that they continue the effort to better their understanding of English without our being forced to completely surrender to this type of cultural ransom?

I wish I'd continued to cultivate my earlier understanding of the languages spoken by my parents. Today I am so very mono linguistic – sad, but true. Still, I am a great proponent of promoting multi language skills in our grade and high schools. This I feel would provide our children greater opportunities in the fields of international trade and commerce. Even as important, in dealing socially and economically with all the newcomers who, regardless of eventual restrictions, will continue to look at our shores as the gateway to a much better life. However, to all you newcomers, remember, English is our national language. Learn it as best you and your children can and don't disparage the need to become proficient. With this added ability comes the advantages you and your supporters constantly demand. I myself attempted to successfully wend my way through semesters of Spanish in college, back in the academic Stone Age I dwelled. Other than my possible inability to learn sufficiently, my major complaint was that the current instruction style at that time, resembled the memorization of the Rosetta stone by the blind and deaf. In addition, our instructors spoke Spanish with the dialect of a Maine lobsterman. Then I tried German but was faced with study material written in a Gothic script not used since Martin Luther pinned his personal opinions on the door of that cathedral in Germany so long ago. And the instructor's pronunciation often resembled speeches one might have heard at early Nuremburg rallies.

The Ever Present 800 Pound Elephant in the Room

Racism has existed in this nation since far before our earliest colonial days – and as disheartening as it may be, will continue in various forms. The black man has suffered over three centuries of abuse, enslavement and the denial of those privileges we all others feel are our natural right. However, let me dictate a very realistic scenario that brought forth the current level of racial discrimination still not as diminished as it should be. For those with even the basics of American history, remember; immediately after the assassination of Abraham Lincoln who truly believed in bringing the nation back together, there arose a force that would become the anti-thesis of harmony and equal opportunity in the southern states, domicile of a majority of blacks. Control fell into the hands of the Democratic Party as they took charge of local and state southern governments. Their acquiescence to the rise of the Ku Klux Klan, more recently one of the party's own leading senatorial figures, himself a former Klan member, created an atmosphere of fear and prohibited the black man any opportunity for free and equal access to that which the white man throughout the country so harbored as his and his alone.

For almost a hundred years, regardless who sat in the White House or the parity or lack thereof between the two political parties in the Congress, the Democrat created and controlled southern bloc - demanded and assured subjugation of the black man. Oddly enough, we never see that bit of history in the demands for equality of the black man, always so prominent in today's leftist campaign rhetoric. Notable that all those clamoring Democrat and other ultra-liberal voices expounding on the deprivation of minority rights, have always seemed to forget that fascinating bit of historical fact. Still, the opposite side of the Congressional aisle, themselves, too frequently allowed this political hostage taking without too loud an objection.

Here's an interesting history for those who found that subject left unserved wherever they went to school, such as Harvard, Yale, Princeton, Columbia and other institutions of higher education nearer the sunny beaches of California. The 13th Amendment abolished slavery with a 100% Republican vote and 23% Democratic support. The 14th Amendment gave citizenship to freed slaves with a 94% Republican backing but 0% from the Democratic Party. To complete this trilogy of revelation to those heralding the support of the black man by one political group over the other, the 15th Amendment gave the right to vote for all men, receiving a hundred per cent support by the Republicans and little if any support from across the aisle. Liars may figure but figures don't lie.

The majority of Americans want to see definitive methods to correct the numerous avenues of opportunity, blocked by an insensitive and posturing legislature. However, that is the role of Congress, the President and the black community leadership itself. It is here where the African-American, (see I've finally used the politically correct term), is so badly served. The assumed spokes people who declare themselves the voice of the black community, are themselves racist of the worst order. There is the constant haranguing by the bellicose and deceptive, shrimp like Al Sharpton, the bigoted blathering of Jesse Jackson, Jr., along with the feculent outpourings of Louis Farrakhan, the head of the American born "Nation of Islam." You will note I didn't call Al Sharpton, "reverend", which would be like calling Jeffrey Dahmer a chef. These three cretins of churlish cacophony, bellow forth their own version of prejudice when needing to enable their constituency to greater support – particularly in a fiscal sense. They merely issue pale platitudes while engendering their personal position and purse, coupled with Congress' own hapless inability to address this problem succinctly.

Do I have any answers to this racial dilemma – well here goes, but again, only my personal view of the situation? Demand black men honor their responsibility, financially and through a degree of parenting, if at all possible, for all those children, legitimate or not. They leave so many young women to support themselves, with children, alone and with limited resources. Require well paid and highly trained teachers in the various schools where the population is evidently minority dominant. Provide funds for the arts and culture, athletics, advanced attention to learning disabilities and school structures that are more than just improperly designed housing for the lesser advantaged.

More effective could be a positive utilization of the black music artists, the "rappers", the "gangsta" lyricists and the many other African American celebrities, to whom the youth of every black community, look to as the ultimate mentor. Near God like in their stature, our youth are mimicking and accepting whatever these synthetic entertainment notables put forth as the mantra of the new generation. Were they to instead, instruct their young followers on adult behavior, the need to create a future through hard work, education and better yet, a respect for each other, the feminine gender, the older generation, the law and particularly their parents and authority figures who strive to assist them in their journey into tomorrow, very possibly the levels of incarceration could decrease.

The major value to rap music is you can't whistle it. The bastardization of the music industry in certain genres, the appealing images of those who defy tradition and normalcy to a degree of criminality, are the sights and sounds too dominant in those youth's view of what they want or should be. So many foolish people, transformed into blathering idiots and self-aggrandizing incompetents, when they have mistakenly accorded themselves talent that is totally non-existent. Regrettably such wanabee', musical misfits become celebrities – a subject to be later discussed. Vaunted heroes to the mentally mismatched – rather, pimples on the buttocks of absurdity.

We have become mired in a constant effort by liberal elements in both political parties, to exponentially increase the entitlement element of present society. However, more the standard campaign tactic of the group who postures as their symbol the long eared mammals smaller that the related horse – otherwise commonly referred to as an ass. On one hand, this party pursues the belief that it is the government's role to provide totally, with inevitable elimination of personal productivity and capitalism. And to the politician, merely a sure way to increase voting blocs, dependent on the ruling party to provide all these benefits at taxpayer costs. However, a simple axiom, never to be forgotten. Whatever the government gives you has to be taken from somebody else.

Before the more liberal reader rises to the Democrat's defense, it must be agreed, the other side of the aisle, those Republican controlled legislatures, have often, during their primacy, constantly thwarted seeming compromise with partisan rhetoric. So there is a decent share of criticism for both sides – the fifty plus shades of blame – aha! I've finally been able to bring in one of Hollywood's latest obvious sequences in obscenity, currently referred to as the edgier darkness of human emotion. Oh, to those with degrees from the numerous liberal bastions of misguided higher education or too many sniffs of the bong, that is a reference to "Fifty Shades of Grey" and it's equally obvious paean to the prurient minded – the sequel.

But one problem still exists – hunger and poverty of our young. It has been reported that 20% of our children either go to bed hungry each night or do not know when their next meal will occur. We spend billions to feed the poor, destitute and oppressed all over the globe, a wonderful example of the American belief in helping where they can, their fellow man elsewhere. Yet, we have children starving here. Families who can barely survive with little hope or opportunity for diminishing their impoverished state. Attention Congress and all you liberal advocates of the one world philosophy, how about a few billion dedicated to our own? For example, Bill Gates, reports of your sending millions to Africa to feed children there while our own here suffer the constant pangs and despair of malnourishment. Or has your avidity to aid others beyond our borders hindered your vision of the evident needs here in your own country?

This is an abysmal stain on our reputation as the freest and most progressive nation in the world. My suggestion, regarding the need to fund those truly in need, instead of automatically raising taxes on the very wealthy, demanding higher rates merely to further fill the coffers of the political vultures and cause further migration of our industries overseas with no resultant benefit, try this suggestion. The large corporate entities, those billionaires and the wealthy of the entertainment and athletic worlds; guarantee a particular percentage or share of yearly profits to be administered by a private entity agreed upon by those providing the funds. Bill Gates, Warren Buffet, youthful multi-millionaire Mark Zuckerberg and the sports world's vociferous bore, Mark Cuban, just to name a very few. People who are successful in their own financial empires and who could assure the monies supplied, would go directly into meals for children, clothing and shoes where needed, an ability to enjoy some recreation and a decent early schooling in the basic means to survive; language, math, reading and an understanding of the nation in which they live.

However, a warning. Do not allow a governmental agency to be involved or all the proceeds will go back down that rabbit hole known as the federal budget. And even more dangerous, ever allowing such pseudo charities like the Bill, Hillary and Chelsea Clinton foundation to get their hands on any of the money, or it too will disappear like a whisper in the wind. Unless of course Bill and Hillary would wish to direct no less than one half of their exaggerated speaking fees to my recommended organization – that is without having any more to say about it than to sign the check. The Clinton Foundation, as the result of the recent national election, may find themselves askance at the quickly diminishing flow of donations from both personal and governmental entities throughout the globe – all assured such endowments would allow them a much smoother entry into the inner coils of the White House and access to the Lincoln bedroom. But that is a matter for others to conjecture – or investigators to continue pursuit.

With the fast rising influx of non-English speaking migrants, we are faced with the increasing demand to find effective ways to teach so many with so little translatable resources. Recently a report stated that in one New York City school of five hundred and eighty students, forty-two separate languages are spoken. Not a sign of diversity. Rather, the potential for the total breakdown of the American educational system. I personally witnessed this phenomenon when visiting one of our local middle schools, on a project for a company I represented, I saw the gaily decorated sign just inside the lobby. "57 different languages are spoken in our school." When I commented on its rather surprising fact, a school official smilingly exclaimed that by the next year that should increase to over 60.

Rushing to the Sound of Gunfire

Sadly, the recent spate of police involved incidents where citizens have either been inappropriately treated or in certain instances, killed, brings forth the continuing need for a revised law enforcement approach to the minority communities. But until the minority community leadership agrees to become more associated with their local law enforcement, to attempt to relate, one to another as equals rather than as adversaries, we will continue to have these tragic and uncalled for incidents of either law enforcement insufficiency or an innate fear of any authority by the individual being approached.

One irrefutable fact is the totally irresponsible and dangerous practice of handing any individual a gun and a badge and the accompanying authority to accost, pursue and/or arrest without proper training and ongoing psychological testing and observation by credited professionals. Too often we find the intensely stress filled and sensitive nature of fulfilling the duties of sworn law enforcement, placed in the hands of those ill prepared to accept such assignments. Individuals with preset bias toward certain ethnic minorities and enamored with the bloated sense of power over his or her fellow citizen must be ferreted out. We cannot expect the Rule of Law and the constitutionally protected rights of all. Everyone, regardless of ethnicity, minority status, evident economic disparity or by nature, seemingly not in the traditional notion of normality, to be provided the fullest measure of their rights when we allow acquisition, meagerly trained and potentially psychopathically challenged individuals emplaced as the guardians of those protections.

Let us face a primary flaw in the entire local law enforcement scenario. The ridiculously low pay and inadequate training, followed by lack of any effective, ongoing evaluation merely strengthens the people's distrust in their local and regional law enforcement. To grant that type of stress filled obligation and do so at wages that barely border the poverty level is in many communities, political chicanery. To the black community, the African American police officer is just another "Uncle Tom," an ill thought misnomer, erroneously created years ago and perpetuated by such racist rabble rousers like Sharpton and Jackson, Jr. and proliferated by the insouciance of the President and the incompetency of his current Department of Justice hierarchy.

Lamentably, one of the most daunting barriers to appropriate investigation of any type of police oriented or allied incident is the black "brother" syndrome. Where those who may have actually viewed a situation with either refused to say anything that could point the legal finger at another black individual, a "brother" or "sister", thus protecting their own. A refusal so often declared publicly.

Death creates the same shocking result. Loss of someone dear to someone else and marked by the presence of blood – whose color over the millennium has never changed from red. Until the refusal to cooperate with investigators and rational cognizance of whatever fact are available, we will see each such event another clarion call for additional reform by the left and the movement of the black community into the Impenetrable fortress of resistance created by the constant effusive vitriol by the self-endowed "black leadership", both activist groups and the political figures seeking greater constituency influence. The minority members of the community must cooperate in becoming part of that legally mandated posture where it is truth and necessary information that is desired . . . not the silence considered acceptable in order to remain part of the environment in which such incidents may occur.

Yet correcting that particular aspect of law enforcement, the extended training, the ongoing oversight and evaluation and much needed wage increases to attract the potential best would create possible sharp tax increases in many smaller rural and urban jurisdictions. One can just imagine the howls of irate citizens and business owners who may themselves never been the victim of a crime and thus, have little or no experience with the call for police assistance. So, without recognition and implementation of these factors, we will continue to see the Fergusons, the Baltimore's and other like sites of turmoil, conflagration, violent protest and the loss of property and regrettably, additional lives.

Our police departments are the symbol of those guaranteed freedoms from fear of assault, theft and invasion of our homes and work places. By allowing the lowered levels of personnel acquisitions, and to minimize the needed training and proper operational oversight, is to allow crime to overshadow every human, social and economic activity. Yet, rather than gathering human and social resources to correct the inherent flaws in certain laxities faced by our law enforcement to, what do we see emanating from certain factions of the minority community –brutal retaliation. The murder of police officers merely exercising their responsibility. Of course, unless the victim was of that same minority classification – silence from those ostensibly the voices of the minority community. This innate hypocrisy was created by the constant reference to a past day when such inequality was a too common and generally accepted norm. It has long been the clarion outburst of those who find it more effective as a political or social activist benefit than any assistance to the true recipients of any such governmental, law enforcement or economic abuse.

As a brief return to an earlier subject, I too have argued both sides of the Electoral College system. It was designed many years ago, to protect the privileged classes from the potential control by a majority of the plebeian masses, according to the review of the original drafters by numerous academicians. Many in our country feel those individuals seeking public office should face the daunting task of acquiring as many votes as possible, both in the primary contests and the eventual national election through acquisition of the largest public acceptance. Simply put, he or she who garners the most votes wins that particular election. One voter, one vote. That anything different in concept tor design violates the individual right to select our leadership.

A selection method not impinged upon by the current electoral system. Anything that distorts that right of the people to participate directly in choosing of their President is an anathema to the intent of our Constitution. Will there ever truly be a one citizen – one vote system? That is for you, dear voters of the future, to decide. Of course, in thinking about the entire electoral process, I've never been able to understand why we have just two people running for President, yet fifty compete for Miss America.

But, faithful reader, an evident caveat must be attached to my idealistic viewpoint. It is also very evident that a straight individual voter process would create another, equally dangerous situation. The urban metropolitan New York City area, the already morally defunct Chicago political system and the bizarre flotsam of Los Angeles and the San Francisco areas, along with a few other major population locations, would normally control the vote. So the conflict in reasoning remains.

On one side is an antiquated system that can and has been manipulated. To the obverse side, potential automatic control by those particular areas and included states, in return for their political loyalty and inevitable governmental fiscal largesse, would assure them all the federal funding possible for the successful elected officials to provide. Thus our new electoral system would merely be the eligible voter lists from approximately a dozen population centers. The Montana's, Utah's, Nebraska's, much of the upper Midwest and upper New England, including certain parts of the south, would be politically omitted from choosing the next president. We are a composite national population, divided by mistrust, lack of confidence in our leadership and never ending fear of the unknown, so true at the time this is being written.

Ready for a brief soiree down the mathematical rabbit hole of election demographics? If not, you can jump a paragraph or two and miss a tasty morsel of statistical fact that could be interesting subject matter for your next political discussion with friends. Using the most recent population estimates as of the time of this writing, July, 2016, nine states, California, Texas, Florida, New York, Pennsylvania, Illinois, Ohio, Georgia and North Carolina, enclose over fifth-one percent of the US population. Add Michigan, New Jersey and Virginia and that figure rises to sixty percent.

Another interesting tidbit from the archives of the U.S. Census Bureau; those first nine states control two hundred forty three of the minimum two hundred seven Electoral votes needed to gain the White House. When attached to the previously mentioned three states, that figure leaps to two hundred and eight six electoral votes. For those graduated from Harvard or its colleague colleges in the East, that totals fifty three percent of the total Electoral College votes. Now, before the liberal left and their associates bring down the ghosts of Martin Luther King, Jr. and the entire civil rights movement, my next presentation will speak to the influence of the two principal minorities in reference to a national vote in contrast to the electoral votes. I speak of the African-American and Hispanic/Latino population. Nothing biased or intended to demean these wonderful people, but the following figures have far more fact than assumption.

If gathered as a singular block, such as the Democrat Party has long envisioned, they represent, considering the twelve states mentioned, over thirty-five percent of that particular voting group. So what do these numbers conclude or prove – very significant if your campaign strategy is aimed principally at the major urban areas where the dominant factors include both numbers and minority configuration. Now that I have possibly confused some, and perhaps bored others, let me leave the decision of how we should vote for our nation's Chief Executive to those who either have the intellectual prowess or the political insight to determine.

Off to Battle the Nine Robed Hierarchy

The United States Supreme Court decided in the affirmative, the question; "Is same-sex marriage a Constitutional right?" The High Court has decided. In the interim they have failed to rule on the demand by certain groups that if any business or service whose religious beliefs prohibits their participation in requests to service various gay requested, e.g. – bakeries, photographers, flower shops – to name just a few examples, be forced to accede to such demands, such refusal be prohibited. The hotly contested subject of same-sex marriage, the recognition of transgender rights to government supported medical services and the continuing demand by LGBT groups for equal representation at all public events, parades, etc. has polarized the nation. In a country where a reported 70% either devoutly or at least nominally consider themselves religious, this will undoubtedly continue to engender controversy regarding what exactly is marriage. Of course, it's often been said that marriage is the major cause of divorce. Among the millennials and the synthetic effete of Hollywood, marriage has become just one of the convenience markets on the way to that super deli of starlet dalliances so common these days.

Added to that decision was one following, wherein the High Court stated that certain controversial interpreted wordage in the Affordable Care Act, better known as "Obamacare", did not prohibit the act from continuing its processing of soliciting potential clients. Whether it survives the efforts of the current administration to continue in any form, however indistinct, is still to be determined. Furthermore it has increased intense focusing on the actual nature of the Supreme Court and what a number of critics observe as a greater legislative input – according to the dissenters, in violation of Article III of the Constitution. The portion that describes the role of the Judiciary as part of the national tripartite as originally conceived by our founding Fathers. However, we will come back to the present position and nature of that nine member shadow legislature.

Now on to far more controversial and angst ridden subjects. How do I consider the ongoing debate regarding the nature of marriage? Very little, if any. At this writing I have been married to a wonderful woman for over 56-years, herself an accomplished athlete and recognized artist of measurable talent. We've raised three children, all successful in their individual ventures. They've provided my wife and me beautiful, talented grandchildren and great grandchildren. Since I've enjoyed such a wonderful family and life, I don't need the aggravation and stress of being a spokesperson for all the ills of the world. I am satisfied people are free to do as they wish, so long as it does not intrude on my personal and Constitutional rights. I leave such mundane quandaries to those who have the time and personal angst to delve into such matters. Those considerations are for me to consider in the privacy of my home and not publicly bloviate, such as is the continuing practice of those paranoid pundits' and political wunderkinds who desire recognition for viewpoints of little value and vacuous content.

For my younger childhood, a momentary recollection. I was the result of a brief coupling of two disparate individuals, most likely just seeking a brief escape from hackneyed lives they neither cherished nor desired to continue without a measure of extracurricular involvement with to whom they were not legally entangled. In those days such pairings were hidden in the dark recesses of whatever forbidden lair held hospitality for such undertakings. In those days my unofficial identification would be bastard; later the term altered by self-serving social advocates to read illegitimate. Regardless of the designation, it was for many years the inevitable "mark of Cain" until Hollywood, and the New York elitist crowd, made producing such legally unattached children the latest fad and have continued the fashion ever since.

I was one of those far more fortunate, adopted at age six by two of the most wonderful people in the world. My adopted father, as I related earlier, arrived from Europe, worked hard and earned his economic way and acceptance by his fellow citizens through honest effort. How that ethical approach has deteriorated in recent decades, I leave to the dome headed, academic quacks who fill the newsprint and airwaves with their nonsensical blather.

My adopted mother was a veritable fortress, protecting the needs of our family. A woman who would put the current, highly publicized female symbols of self-assurance and personal strength to shame. My father's death when I was thirteen was a loss I don't believe she ever fully overcame. But by her sheer willpower and sense of obligation to her son and the farm on which we lived, we prevailed. My father was just four months short of twenty-five years at the steel mill where he'd been considered a valued employee. But as was not uncommon in those days, the company hierarchy contended he'd not reach the mandatory pension level required - but we prevailed.

Living a dozen miles from the city where my father's family resided, she experienced the common factor among many ethnic cultures and communities. Her family was miles away in another state. True she was part of the overall related family structure, having married one of its male members. But she was not really "family" in the normal sense of the word. An outsider, in a manner after her husband died, she prevailed and became a successful operator of a small hospice location for the elderly infirmed. When I read or hear the laudatory gushing of the media over the claimed uniqueness of the Oprahs', the Martha Stewarts, Hillary the perennial candidate, political activist Elizabeth Warren and the other ersatz nobility of modern day feminism, they're wimps. You want to know what a real woman was. You want to see personal strength and purpose, you should have met my adopted mother. Now there was a fighter, a righteous force to respect."

Again, To the Battle with Pen and iPad

Back to the media, print, broadcast and the highly evolved electronic transmission via "Instagram" and "Twitter", that medium too often misused by our current President.   Not to forget that addiction of the modern age, "Facebook." We are being told by those who earn their living preaching the technological tripe that merely enhances the income of the Japanese and Chinese electronic combines, that soon robots will replace many human workers. Could happen, I suppose. However, it would be no fun kicking a robot in its software package when they screw up or become laggardly in completing their function or listening to their union shop steward more than you. What should one do when the machine doesn't warrant employment anymore because it has failed to meet your expectations? Say, "you're fired", unhook its hard drive and tell it to report to the recycling bin?

I'm sure there is benefit to the communication accessibility, yet one factor remains predominant. Totally divulging your life, your thoughts, your every activity and deepest feelings on Facebook, is much like leaving your front and back doors open. Even more so, posting a sign; "come on in", I have nothing to hide, nothing of personal value I wish to keep safe from prying eyes and those with evil intent. Twitter is the verbal belching of the ill-informed and the emotionally repressed, the vocal conduit for the reckless recluse. The plethora of online dating sites may too often merely be invitations of opportunity for potential rapists, thieves, pedophiles, frauds and scams. Such websites were developed for the unsure about their personal insecurity in a world about which they are unprepared to face in a mature and rational manner, regardless the difficulties.

The national news today is often ill equipped to understand its adulterated content has been, over the past three decades, merely a propaganda outlet, either for the stalwart and dedicated Democratic Party membership or the ever increasingly ultra-liberal segment of our populace – there I go again - I have erred. Those two recipients of the major media's overblown love fest are not separate. Rather, they are coupled like modern day Bonnie & Clyde's – forever entwined in their respective hate for anything traditional, normal or even slightly conservative in viewpoint or approach.

When I was in the School of Journalism at a large Midwestern University, one of my senior professors was very emphatic regarding a particular mandate, which more than once, he voiced after seeing one of my reports on some local or governmental meeting, submitted as a class assignment. He said, as I remember and with no caveats, "When and if you are ever paid specifically for your personal opinion, in any column or report, then you may do so. Until then, your function is to report; facts, happenings and comments from relevant and pertinent witnesses or respondents – nothing more. Otherwise you will have crossed that thin line between objectivity and bias."

I never forgot that caution. So disheartening, that this line is crossed every day in print and over the airwaves and through the technological wonder of television. Primped young ladies, definitely positioned to be ogled by the male viewer, while possibly dissented by the female viewers. As to the other side of the anchor desk, coiffured presenters with male model presence. But let us not forget the tabloid writer or cable news investigator, more like a drunken gunslinger, walking down the street, shooting out the windows on both sides out of sheer enjoyment to have the right.

We miss the classic news voices of the past. They've been replaced by TV's "talking heads", as has been humored in numerous comedic dialogue. On the print side, pages of supposed on site and personal interviews with political and other of the celebrity genre, become nothing more than either personalized aggrandizement of or an attempt to vilify the subject. Particularly if that subject espouses a policy or viewpoint in opposition to the standard liberal opinion.

There are few electronic and print voices who attempt to bring fairness and completeness to every reportorial effort. Sadly, they are too often the butt of progressive oriented comedy routines or vitriolic response from their peers on the other more "enlightened" outlets. The renowned broadcast legend Edward R. Murrow once wrote, "Many people think they are thinking when they are merely rearranging their prejudices."

What can be done? Nothing in reality, until the leftist oriented and insufficiently conditioned instructors in the major educational institutions, are replaced by those who truly believe in teaching the traditional ethics of journalism. That suggestion will undoubtedly be quickly disavowed by the Ivy League and society of surfing studs encompassed in the major California educational institutions.

Now to quickly review the major proponents of journalistic supremacy. The fabled New York Times, once considered by many of the more literate as the herald of free speech and assuring the truth always be paramount, has as its masthead, "All the news that's fit to print." Today it could read, "All the news that fits after editing out the facts." Other major urban publications in Los Angeles, San Francisco, Chicago, Boston and Washington, seem to follow that path and the list seems endless. Even my own local publication, the Salt Lake Tribune, has become the layered pulp purveyor for a continuing deluge of far left viewpoint on almost every subject, one might feel, merely parroting the intent of its resident, publisher. Its principal cartoonist consistently displays a rather convoluted and antithetical approach to facts, more often than not constantly insulting the subject in his presentations.

I have long wondered if he is merely off his medication or suffers ongoing recollections of early child abuse.

Sadly, print journalism is slowly dying the inevitable death of reduced subscriber strangulation. A tightening of costs and growing use of digital news gathering. The never ceasing growth of receiving ones information, music and movies through the modern technology of "streaming", has doomed the traditional newspaper. Once over 1800 dailies flourished throughout the country. Today, less than four hundred have survived.

As to the rank and file of television, the three supposed major networks, NBC, ABC and CBS, have too often become repositories of slovenly declared fairness and constantly butchered event substance to please the God of ratings. Their early morning, wannabe celebrity laden host lists have instituted a constant babble of voices, impossible to understand what any individual is saying. As for entrepreneurial broadcast maven, Ted Turner's CNN, it struggles, but still remembered as the first – the progenitor of the many such cable outlets now in place - although more lately, having joined the meaningless trivia of their fellow cable cohorts. MSNBC is termed by its many critics as a broadcasting joke, a parody of the pointless and absurd. Its correspondents so biased as to make each utterance more embarrassing to the rational viewers.

Several of the principal TV cable news program hosts, for lack of any other more practical description of their sophomoric commentaries, are sycophantic pretenders. MSNBC's Chris Matthews, who couldn't listen to an Obama speech without a chill going down his leg – very possibly just a continuing regrettable bladder problem from too much coffee. Perhaps a leaking colostomy bag. And not to forget the boring bitch of broadcasting, Rachel Maddow, who, if she weren't a paid performer on that channel, might have a difficult time filling in as a female cigar store Indian. Again, as long as these broadcast companies insist on kneeling at the altar of ultra-liberal devotion, we can expect little improvement in their ability to be fair. As a note to Mr. Matthews and Ms. Maddow – who might wish to respond, it's the First Amendment I have employed if your attorneys attempt to threaten me for disparaging their clients. And not to omit the diminutive George Stephanopoulos, now a highly touted member of the ABC news punditry . . . but once former President Bill Clinton's adoring "gofer". One of the White House munchkins during that administration.

Fox News proclaims they are the only "fair and balanced" news and commentary coverage. However, they are also accused of impinging on that line between the objective and the biased. As to their standing in the polls, I leave that to the rating gurus. At the polar opposite to numerous other more liberal outlets, sat TVs Bill O'Reilly, most lately exiled to the Siberia of sexual harassment accusations. And the acerbic, Sean Hannity, along with a variable selection of male and female proponents of a far more conservative viewpoint. My opinion, O'Reilly's principal flaw was his seeming refusal to allow anyone being interviewed to finish a sentence. He stated many times, "it is his program," which avoids the need to be objective without insistence on only his viewpoint unless the guest immediately agrees with his version of the subject. However he has become part of either the past or entered some pantheon of the ultra-right since his recent dismissal from Fox programming which reportedly cost his employer a bundle just a few years ago. Thus, he went the way of Elliot Spitzer, former Governor of New York and former senator John Edwards, once a presidential candidate, more lately, NBC's Matt Lauer, actor Kevin Spacey and again, the roll call continues. Too many allowing their testosterone level to overcome their voter appeal.

Although, Fox News, Sean Hannity, has a lengthy record of conservative viewpoints, his haranguing on certain subjects and evident support on air of the Trump candidacy, was his right as a citizen but his program should have possibly displayed the caveat that his broadcast was a personalized commentary – not a general discussion format.

It is a sad commentary that Fox news constantly inserts the biased and self-aggrandizing comments of Juan Williams, their token minority who became an outspoken apologist for Barack Obama. Of course others are brought on to espouse the standard Democratic retort to anything said by any other participant when discussing recent White House verbal convolutions. Last, another pseudo minority entrant, Geraldo Rivera, who insists on having ideologically suspect opinions regardless the subject. Some anonymous twits years ago opined he was originally called Jerry Rivers. But when the sudden rise of Latino culture impacted national broadcasting . . . voila! Geraldo Rivera arrived. Perhaps just another of the rampant rumors or undisguised slur that prevail in the world of supposed celebrities. For many, radio has its Rush Limbaugh, hefty figured master of the talk format for a quarter of a century, reportedly still holding the largest audience rating in the industry. His critics have long voiced their opposition to his dialogues against the formidable wall of broad public acceptance. But like the bookie getting rich off the betting populace, "he's got the numbers."

Without Caution, Entering the Legal Lair Once More

I shall now again dash forward in this diatribe, to cast my personal opinion regarding another sacred icon of our nation, the august United States Supreme Court and their lesser judicial underlings. The obvious contorted role of the judiciary in recent years is a pet peeve of mine. Our Founding Fathers formulated a governmental structure in three parts. The Executive Branch that oversees the national interest, particularly in the area of global relations, the defense of our shores and is sworn to uphold the Constitution as it exists during his or her term. The Legislative branch is comprised of those elected representatives whose responsibility is to develop and present annual budgets, pass required laws and other involvement with pertinent issues affecting their constituencies. It is the obligation of the judiciary, headed by the nine members of the High Court, to assure that any law proposed, passed or contested, follows the dictate and intent of the Constitution. It is this expression, "intent", that creates the continual whirlwind of criticism of the High Court's seemingly apparent move toward creating law rather than adjudicating its relativity and correctness to the situation or complaint as presented.

It appears more and more that the High Court and to a lesser degree certain lower courts, are attempting to create social policy. That is not their responsibility, nor their right, as enumerated in Article III of the Constitution. In pursuing this direction, they would be, in fact, usurping the guarantees of fair and equitable distribution of power between the three mandated branches of government. However, as we are all well aware, there is no protocol for their removal, save finding them in bed with a dead girl or a live boy. Or possibly, spending their summer vacation period in an ISIS, Jihadist training camp somewhere in Iran.

Associate Justice, Thurgood Marshall, once stated, "You do what you think is right and leave the law to catch up." A dangerously thin defense of assuming a legislative right not specified in the Constitution. Interestingly, many of these justices attended Harvard, Columbia or Princeton. There, we have provided a brief and concise review of the tripartite form of our government, which I fear is possibly more than that already included in the yearly abbreviated textbook versions in most schools. Such details being considered academically too heavy for our future voters by the ultra-liberal schoolboard overseers. The Executive Branch faced my wrath earlier, but not to fear, additional comments will be forthcoming. The Legislative Branch will feel the sharpness of my pen later. For now, we target the currently seated "High Court." They are to be the watch guards of our founding document. Their function is to avoid obfuscation of that document's wordage in favor of one side over another without valid reason.

But to this writer, the members in their black robes at the time of this writing, continue to disrespect the mandated division of labors and responsibilities the three part structure of our government requires. They appear to interpret or consider development of new concepts in a manner that in fact, seems to create markedly revised law – which is not their right. If what they determine within the context and current language of the Constitution to be in variance of what is being proposed or litigated, then a refreshed legal interpretation may occur. But to take it on themselves to rewrite an existing law and use their judicial position to offset, or disregard the position of the Legislative Branch without return for possible correction by that body, is misfeasance. Simply the performance of a lawful act in an illegal or improper manner. They are legislating, not adjudicating as their many critics will stipulate regarding a number of their recent decisions, referred to earlier.

With the aging of the court, new potential appointments could easily shift the High Court far toward one pole or the other. The newest president is presently able to shift that balance in nominating a more conservative member. One recent appointee, under the former Obama banner, spoke strongly of her opinion that ethnic, cultural and economic insufficiency should color the administration of the rule of law. Another relatively recent member, who had no experience on any bench and was, in fact, the official legal solicitor for the President appointing her – veritably a mirror of his philosophy and liberal legal leanings. That both are female is of no consequence other than rightfully providing our legal review a greater presence by the opposite gender. It is hoped these two members will remember the writings of Edmund Burke, 18th Century Anglo-Irish statesman, when he penned, "Bad laws are the worst of tyranny."

If the most current administration were to retain the White House for another four to eight years, it is feasible an additional two to four court appointments would occur. That would create a Supreme Court far to the right, in a more conservative position to ostensibly, per its proponents, thwart a liberal influence for the next several decades.

Only time will tell. With the death of Associate Justice Antonin Scalia last year, the court remained at four – four. The newest confirmed member, notably far more right than left, has once more changed the balance. It is the role of the High court to be the protector of our revered Constitution. However, there is a quote, ascribed to the Roman Poet Juvenal, and at times literally revised, "Quis custodiet ipsos custodies." "Who will guard the guardians?" So without further adding to the destruction of more trees in continuing this particular subject, let us proceed down another road.

A Venture into the Financial Fiasco

The present economic crisis facing this country, at the time of this writing, has shocked the current fiscal Fagin's' of Charles Dickens fame, overwhelmed the politicians and impoverished many of the public. Yet when the government created financial institutions known familiarly as Freddie Mac and Fannie Mae, they were allowed to engage in highly risky investments and mortgage procedures. To provide low interest rates to many desirous home buyers, all well-intentioned but proven to have meagre if insufficient capability to repay the increased monthly notes. Where were the restraints to such excessive abuse of reason? The two Congressional scoundrels who were major supporters of these abuses were Senator Chris Dodd and Rep. Barney Frank, the mincing minion of the Dodd/Frank Act, who when the financial chaos was recognized, immediately cloaked themselves in self-professed ignorance of the monetary misdeeds. Lately their remaining congressional cohorts have sponsored more seemingly restrictive controls on the mortgage industry. However, in the name of political expediency, the new regulations have already been adulterated with extensive omissions and waivers for special interests. Sounds much like the hangman apologizing to the accused that he only had a used rope available.

Never in this later history of our country have our legislators achieved so little with so much effort to impede any accomplishment through their personal inability to accomplish anything worthwhile. There, my quick diagnosis of Congress.

I am bothered, during these dire times, to read the constant news reports of cities, counties and states needing to eliminate or reduce their law enforcement, fire and emergency medical resources in order to establish a working budget. We face a burgeoning federal budget and a horrendously bloated government work force, immune from any substantive punishment or discipline for deeds done bad or incompetency on the job. The reason, simple, federal, state and local employees unions have handicapped and literally destroyed any chance to correct the ensuing poor management, laxity in proficiency, internal fraud and overt extravagance in the administration of government on all levels.

As you might expect, I have a suggestion. To all those elected and appointed financial supervisors, whether in Washington, any state capitol or local administration, here's a quick resolution. Roam the halls and offices of your various administrative headquarters. Take note of all those folks requiring constant bathroom breaks, quick smoke outings and those with cell phones constantly glued to their ears, obviously hiding the true intent of their conversations. Or who spend excessive time in idle chatter with fellow inmates, possibly those continuing to surreptitiously access the latest in online pornography. That mélange who never accomplish any assigned task within a reasonable time frame.

Carry a pad of the proverbial pink slips, have the power to immediately reprimand, use suspensions without pay or eventual dismissal for those egregiously affecting the viability and effectiveness of their assigned functions. And to the Congress, those mandated to act on the behalf of the people, pass laws making such intolerable excess foisted on us by an unwarranted obeisance to the federal, state and teacher's union cartel, unacceptable and subject to immediate recourse. Install the expression, "terminated" or suspended "without pay" within the primary lexicon of future administrative procedures.

The problem – the proven insurmountable barrier to such responsible management control – dollars! The massive sums flowing from union coffers to campaign cash stressed politicians. Saving the citizen's tax input would mean less dinaros' for their vault to higher elected office.

It's been reported over fifty five percent of all designated union members are within local, state and national government workforces. Their opportunity to filch from the public coffers with this type of control must be lessened. Their contract structure permits abuses and absolute immunity for members, often from any slightest form of discipline or correction. This outrageous exercise of a power, never originally intended, has cast stain on the history of those who earlier, courageously fought for the union movement that allowed the American worker a voice in his or her own future in the workplace.

The major industrial and service unions had in the past fought their own internal corruption, but they survived and took it on themselves to correct many of their deficiencies. Sadly, a large portion of the member dues required are still too often directed toward only those political candidates who advocate the principle policies of the Democratic Party.

Today the history of the true labor movement's tumultuous beginning has been all but shelved in the dusty archives of human memory. The Milwaukee Iron Company strike, or Bay View Massacre when Wisconsin National guard shot and killed seven strikers, including a 13-year old boy. And the Pittsburgh Homestead Strike of 1892 and the infamous Colorado Ludlow Massacre of 1914. Those were horrific periods in early labor's history. They deserve to be part of the history taught our youth. But in doing so, there has to be remonstrance to the traditional union organizations, that the same youths being taught the history of early union struggles can be assured that past graft and internal corruption has, or will, end. Conjecture, perhaps pure yearning, but still the goal desired to overcome past transgressions

These public employee unions are no longer legitimate assurances for worker rights. They are merely vote enabling and campaign funding resources. They have too often become legally authorized and taxpayer supported housing for the incompetent, the indolent and the potentially corrupt, as they continue to undermine the traditional and constitutionally mandated obligations of the government.

The increasing emphasis on using the federal budget as an endless cornucopia to satisfy the folks back home and maintain an inflated bureaucracy, was termed years ago as "political pork." Today it continues to create a stench in the halls of Congress, reminiscent of being downwind from a hog farm on a very hot day in July. Although the employee budget is a resource targeted originally to engender public safety, a resolute defense of our shores and medical care for the people Congress is mandated to serve, it has merely become a method to protect the minimally productive government employees from being forced to find legitimate work and not crowd the unemployment offices.

Try to fire such a protected individual. Possibly a suspension if the figure is too publicly visible, always with pay and benefits continuing. Then, the lengthy time required before a hearing. Now there's an amusing oxymoron. By then, transfer to a less discernible position, or early retirement, still coupled with earned benefits. Again, some animals always seem more equal than others.

The Presidential Parade

Although I have mentioned a principal subject in this following paragraph, I just can't let her fade back into her created aura of personal nobility. I never really liked Bill Clinton, although I will admit, one had to respect and marvel at his polished form of political savvy. An example of doing so many questionable undertakings with little regard or attention by the devoted media. He is the true political savant, who continually emulates the worst attributes of a used car salesman, while being the most efficient practitioner of the political arts in many years. Truly a master of the factual shuffle, he would be able to sell you a '94 dodge auto, assuring you he had personally assured its satisfactory answer to your travel needs. A block away from the sales lot, the engine dies unceremoniously. You return, demanding restitution, only to be assured that it was you who made the inappropriate choice of vehicle. One has to be impressed with his ability to merchandise spoiled legislative product into a semblance of reconstituted value, prepared especially for the believers in his revival tent dictates.

His wife, the perennial public patroness, is eaten with ambition. Her past roles, in the White House as First Lady, later as a Senator through an at best, strange acquisition of state residential eligibility, and later under the current administration as one of the most self-serving and inefficient Secretary of State in the history of that position, created a resume rampant with narcissism. Recent revelations of she and her husband's highly questionable funding approaches and the massive income both have acquired since leaving the Executive Mansion, is reason enough to alter her original title from former First Lady, now to current "shady lady." Interesting that former president, Richard Nixon was accused of erasing 18 ½ minutes of tape while Hillary has been equally charged of possibly deleting thousands upon thousands of emails? And the media immediately called Nixon a crook?

She has, however, again proven that the female of the species, like her Black Widow spider contemporary, has learned to persist, to survive, regardless of the definable cloud of misdeed that constantly surrounds her and her husband. But that's for others to expound upon. The details are too upsetting and morally indigestible to the honest person. I have but one final comment. Bill Clinton's past female conquests and sordid soirees should enable him to become a notable advertising icon for Viagra when all those massive speaking fees dwindle. Her relationship to the Benghazi fiasco, Whitewater funding debacle and of course the highly suspect Clinton Global Initiative whose coffers have burgeoned to a massive degree by donations from sources need more surveillance than auditing.

As to whether she might ever face legal retribution for her roles in the varied accusations, it is doubtful, based on the recent upset loss to the blustering, New York, Tweet obsessed real estate mogul. Still a cloudy horizon, indistinct if her involvement will ever reach any criminal charges. Should the entire matter be ended and merely a part of footnotes in future histories – again, that is for other far more astute to such matters than I. The highly publicized Clinton Foundation, undoubtedly now, as the White House is soon to have another resident, may see the flow of charitable donations from persons and global sites markedly diminished. But, we will let others and time determine that potential.

However, let's not move away from the Hillary Rodham Clinton psyche, just yet. Her life with a husband, referred to by some as "slick willy," yet rising to the most powerful position in the world, the grist for other publishing mills. As her thesis subject at Wellesley College, she wrote on the works of Saul Alinsky, considered founder of modern community organizing. One of Alinsky's comments from his 1971 book, "Rules for Radicals," the literal bible for urban agitation, used by Hillary, was, "Fan the latent hostilities in any group." His rather disputed works were also part of Barack Obama's reading list during his earlier Southside Chicago community organizing efforts. Interesting talking points for a potential, future President of the most powerful country in the world who constantly campaigned on her care for the American middle class.

At this writing a cartoon appeared in our local newspaper. One I've had memorialized under plastic sheeting as it expressed the opinion of so many after her recent electoral debacle. Her post-election book was released in late 2017. The first panel of the brilliantly presented cartoon art, displays her announcing the newest Clinton bloviating. The second states simply, "First Chapter, I Lost. The End."

As stated before, President Barack Hussein Obama was not my choice for President – actually preferring "Soupy Sales," after having reviewed Obama's credentials. But he was the choice via the Electoral College process of which I have spoken earlier He's neither all black nor all white. His mother a Kansan Caucasian and father a Kenyan black. Interesting combination as referred to in a recent book by Pulitzer Prize winning author, David J. Garrow, published just as I was finishing this volume. A massive work detailing many aspects of Obama's early life and eventual rise to celebrity status. The book, "Rising Star" may be the most definitive, but absolutely boring compilation of our past Presidents varied background. Can be put on a bookshelf, better yet, as a doorstop.

But enough of all that minutia of meaningless background. He is now part of a past he helped create and will undoubtedly spend his remaining years, attempting to outdo the indefatigable William Jefferson Clinton as the world's leading senior statesman. Reams of material have already claimed total knowledge of the media's proposed "Black Messiah." So we'll let him pursue his desire to enhance what he long before may have determined to be his rightful legacy. I'll not be around to mark any further ascension of his personal acclimation.

The media's liberal adulation at President Obama's inauguration was continually laced with references to his similarity to Abraham Lincoln's freeing the slaves while facing a controversial war. He continually attempts to echo the vaunted leadership of F.D.R, speaking of his Roosevelt like primary source for hope by the socially and economically oppressed. Let us take another look at that period of American history. Eight years into FDR's reign, the Depression was still a cloud of financial disaster, darkening our skies. As time will always work its mysterious pattern of circumstance, Japan's ill-conceived attack on Pearl Harbor in December, 1941, awakened the sleeping tiger. It propelled us into a global conflict and at the same time it gave genesis to an industrial might and capitalistic posture, a magnificent accomplishment still unequaled in the world despite the current administrations attempt to quell its importance to American prosperity.

Also, complexing to this writer; during Obama's administration cops were being called criminals, criminals were victims, people who don't want to work get immediate assistance, desecrating our flags is acceptable, cross-dressers are called heroes, we supply guns to drug cartels while attempting to disarm all citizens. We are spending millions of dollars and hours of verbal puffery regarding the transgender situation and demand for non-sex defined bathrooms while many children still lack a decent education and enough food to eat. And it was still George W. Bush's fault? Please. Give me a break!

Time will tell, as it always does with the pronouncements of those desiring historic immortality.

However Leonard Pitts, noted African-American columnist for the Miami Herald, wrote an interesting perspective to all this avowed Lincoln connection. He contended, Lincoln didn't actually intend to just free slaves. But rather, his "Emancipation Proclamation," was a military measure to demoralize and destabilize a rebellious south. Furthermore, and most cogent, was, according to Pitts, Lincoln's belief, documented in a 1858 speech, wherein he stated, "There is a physical difference between the white and black races which. . . will forever forbid the two races living together on terms of social and political equality." Lincoln's sole objective was preservation of the Union. Our president and Congress need to remember that salient point when they charge ahead to change the tenor of American morals and traditional values. To assure that what they attempt to create does not in its stead destroy that which we all cherish and has been achieved to date.

We have traveled a long and difficult road to reach at least a degree of the desired equality demanded by so many. But let us forge through those thorny brambles later in this volume. We are now facing possible total recall of the national health reform bill that none of the voting legislators or the president had actually reviewed, and the Speaker of the House at that time, Nancy Pelosi, "brayer from the Bay," had the gall to publicly push for its approval so that, "Its contents could be read." Talk about putting the legislative cart before the horse. I remember years ago when I saw one of my sons reading the novel, "Ali Baba & the Forty thieves as a school assignment. I had to caution him. "Son, you're far too young to study politics."

When Barack Obama became the Democratic candidate for President in 2008, I voted for John McCain, primarily out of loyalty for a fellow veteran and his survival as a prisoner of war. However, inwardly, I felt that this new comer, this charismatic black man, highly articulate, just might be the spur of a resurgence for our nation. Within three months I quickly recognized how badly the electorate had been misled. His Vice-President, with the gift of gaffes was merely extending his congressional pension plan with another eight years at the public trough. What was the old joke line? A woman had two sons, one went to sea as a sailor and the other became Vice President – neither were ever heard from again.

In 2012 I voted for Mitt Romney, an individual I felt had the business acumen and moral and ethical standards to be an effective and incorruptible leader of our country. Ok, so I was part of the management group that he led to such a successful 2002 Winter Olympic Games. He came off as an honest, sincere and warm personality without the vitriolic nature and all-consuming ambition required by someone seeking the ultimate political prize. At this time we have the 45th President, who's every move, every comment, either verbally, or by the infamous Tweeter technology, is torn asunder by a media, still cringing at their role in the loss of the 2016 election by Hillary Rodham Clinton. A blame that must be shared by her total lack of understanding of the ideological tumult raging in the hinterland, coupled with a Democratic Party insensitive to the ridiculous, sophomoric inattention to public concerns. Equally aided by an apparently apathetic Republican conclave – intent on criticism rather than compromise.

I once lived in an eastern city, noted for the ongoing ineptitude and governmental inadequacy – oops! Definitely an oxymoron. One twit commented, "You know, the only real way to correct our problems is to have a few good funerals." Now that might be considered by some as a bit harsh and is probably in conflict with a number of laws, yet, there are some who feel such a course of action within many legislatures might be more productive than reelection. One last jibe at the former Chief Executive at this writing. President Obama was regarded by some as an accomplished speaker, possibly surpassing the eloquence of Reagan, Kennedy or Roosevelt, a pseudo legacy continually touted by an adoring media. However, I fear, if Teleprompters had ever gone out of vogue, Barack Hussein Obama might easily have become speechless.

However, at the writing of this time consuming tome, the current resident of the White House is undergoing media, opposition party, and the self-servers in his own party and of course the inhabitants of those tax supported Ivory Towers, academia, an onslaught unparalleled in the sleazy world of political life. Whether he will survive, who knows? Will he be evicted from 1600 Pennsylvania Avenue? Again, must be left up to all those self-endowed autocrats of social conducts to whom the unlettered are forced to endure and the educated malcontents look to as governmental gurus.

Wandering Through the Newest Wonderland

I've never quite understood why so many younger, supposed celebrities, pen autobiographies of lives they've yet to have spent the years necessary for more than a slight move out of prepubescence. It confuses fact, since they haven't completed enough tasks and goals that should make reading such a short, inconsequential personal history, gratifying. Why is it some entertainment notables, who after just a few months or brief years of success in whatever they do, insist on revealing their supposedly personal secrets in quickly, and primarily ghost written biographies? Overly priced volumes in which they declare their new found wisdom and understanding of a world they have yet resided in so briefly. And during a brief tenure that reflects little if any achievement, other than legions of unsophisticated minions, who find his idolization to be the veritable, singular goal in their vacuous existences.

Apparently it appeals to a readership either too enamored of their idol's accomplishments, or too bored to find truly interesting and substantive viewpoints elsewhere. Upon acquiring the new found wealth from their pop celebrity status, many of these would be entertainment magnets immediately attempt to become pundits on every subject imaginable. While constantly exhibiting a gaudy lifestyle, they instantly become spokespeople for the poor and disadvantaged, ad nauseam. They speak of noble pursuits but with a potentially suspicious intent. Is it truly to support the needy or to support their public relations image? Hypocrisy still abounds in the world of the elite, and their offspring are following faithfully in the same chaotic, genetic paths as their parents or mentors.

When I was much younger, and talk about a real long glance backwards, it seemed so simple to define the good from the bad, the acceptable from the sinful. Heroes were very evident by their stated objective to achieve the good and resist the evil. Evil doers and those not accepted in society were equally without disguise. Perhaps my rather normal youth and somewhat commonplace adulthood, precluded my recognizing the future as so many writers and media pundits claim to have a Nostradamus like ability to perceive what will happen.

Since I'm quickly approaching the end of that long tunnel we all must tread, I become more aware of my compelling desire to speak out – make known for any who would listen or care what I believe – often of no interest to others – sometimes even to myself. We all will move into that eternal darkness that holds whatever future our personal or religious inclination tends to expect. It is still a conundrum that so many fear death, when that it is an occurrence, inevitable of course, but a moment no one truly knows when, and often, how it will happen. To live with that fear is to darken the light of the days still before us. Fear kills imagination and reduces human effort to a defensive posture. It is that regrettably status that precludes us resisting, fighting back against those situation that would make us less willing to face each new day.

As stated earlier, I'm merely a voice from the back of the crowd, waiting for the parade to pass. Autobiographies are normally collections of memories of which I have many in number. Reminiscing is time travel in reverse, a journey without planning, initiated only by the traveler. But I have closeted mine for my personal retrieval and at rare times, to use as platforms for commentary when asked about certain portions of my life. The names of those who have aided my development and provided me much cherished friendships are embedded in my memory, to be remembered and kept as favorite moments during my remaining time.

My beginning in a rural community, vacant the amenities of a more complicated urban life, allowed me to enjoy the relationships that develop with those with whom you've risen through the early years of growth. My classmates at the school in nearby West Chester, Ohio, were the companions of my childhood and friends of my youth. In college, as a member of a major fraternity, Beta Phi Chapter, Delta Tau Delta, they were my associates in scholastic effort, in youthful ribaldry and so often, the inevitable search for the ladies of our dreams. They too are so much a part of my past that I dread time will diminish in visage. And like my earlier classmates, a number of these good comrades have also passed from this earthly domain. I miss them all. Although no longer of a firm religious bent, my personal concept of heaven would be, to one day join all of those who meant so much to me. Someplace where we would all revert to that age when things were good and would never seem to pass.

One fact has remained with me, the need to always accept that how we are viewed by others, often varies strongly, in conflict with our view of our self. Early in my facility management career, while hosting a major ice show event, I had assumed my "floor walker" stance in the lobby, feeling very self-assured in position and status – only in my mind of course. An elderly lady came walking speedily toward me from inside the seating area, waving what appeared to be a ticket stub. She, spotting my coat and tie, and possibly officious posture, stated she wanted to speak to someone with a little authority about her seat location. Recognizing what I may have resembled, I responded. "Madam, speak to me. I have as little authority as anyone around here and feel I'm getting less every day." That has been my personal mantra ever since.

Being a consultant on a number of facility design and management projects, here and abroad, has given me a more expanded view of the world than had I remained in my home location in the southern Ohio farmland. But as insightful and clever I imagined my expertise to be, I've never forgot the description of a consultant, provided me by a friend years ago. He said, "A consultant is some guy who supposedly knows ninety ways of making love, but doesn't know any women." Or as I came to understand eventually, it could be someone who borrows your pen to write you a report on a subject you probably know better than he, charges you an exorbitant fee and then steals the pen he borrowed.

I've come to realize I must now be considered well within the senior population since I keep receiving an ever increasing number of Medicare advertisements, senior living periodicals and the almost monthly notices from local cemeteries and funeral homes offering their specific services. They always promote choice plots still being available, extolling the view from certain preferred locations. As if I should care what vista is most prominent from six feet underground?

From Where Comes the Vision?

I like many others, cloak myself with that vaunted First Amendment and will express my right to free speech. Even more so, I understand and respect those limitations created to avoid overt or inadvertent defamation and slander. Am I prejudiced? About certain things, most assuredly, as are all mankind. Just like all others of my specie, my upbringing and life's experiences has affected me emotionally and emboldened me intellectually. Yet, in that prejudice is a firm desire to correct my thinking as time and my exposure to more modern concepts and needs of my fellow man have come into view.

I've long been an avid reader of history and with a great liking for adventure novels of Ludlum, Brown, Forsythe, Cussler, Berry, Silva and W.E.B. Griffin. And the list goes on. Their splendorous detail of events, places and historicity of mankind intrigues me. My other love, the works of the Russian authors, Tolstoy, Chekhov, Dostoyevsky, Pushkin, Gorky and the more modern Solzhenitsyn. It has long been said, no one writes better of the capacity for suffering and toleration of the abysmal than the Russian author.

We truly miss the great voices of Martin Luther King, Jr., Gandhi, Nelson Mandela and their compatriots who trod the dangerous road to an equality, long forbidden goals sought by them and their followers. King's speech at the Lincoln Memorial was the high water mark of the civil rights cause. Tragically, the deaths and pillaging, burnings, rioting and character assassinations that have followed, have become the sequential low points. The Washington Post had named Barack Obama the third "greatest presidential orator" in the modern age, only behind JFK and FDR. Again, without that constant teleprompter, he might have ranked just behind Calvin Coolidge.

I can never be politically correct as I firmly believe that the current racially espoused social concept is the result of ill-conceived and politically contrived programs, with no hope for achievement. It creates an escutcheon for the advocates of income equality, who themselves wallow at times in unearned or celebrity acquired wealth, far in excess of the many in the "underclass" with whom they so avidly declare allegiance. I claim the right to be biased, if that is the politically correct word. Hopefully, not to excess, to dislike someone, or someplace or something so long as, in that expression or opinion, I am not defaming, insulting, denying an equal retort or the full measure of rights assured everyone in our country. And in being such, I must strive to accept the rights of all, regardless of ethnic, cultural, social, sexual orientation or economic particulars.

Another note of an increasing occurrence. With the growth in our Asian population has regrettably come the equal rise in what are commonly referred to as "Asian gangs." Groups of youths who have become bewitched by the apparent quick and less laborious system for garnering cash and marketable materials, drugs and guns, needed to pursue their criminal activities. Yet, it's a fact, tinged with sadness, that their parents and so many others of their ethnic genealogy, have often proven their productivity in America. Have been part of our miraculous growth over the past two centuries. When reading the list of recent honorees in various fields of science, music, mathematics, etc., many of the winners bear Asian names.

Why, many people ponder is this noticeable ability of our Asian fellow man and those from India, succeed so well? I believe it is their cultural heritage. It is their discipline of achieving and steadfastness in pursuing academic, artistic and more recently, athletic goals. They express in that diligence to achievement, a belief that consistent effort will bring forth the flower of success from what others may consider a barren landscape of opportunity. Theirs is a belief in the sanctity and utmost value of family and devotion to the ideals and traditions they have been taught.

It is this determination, which often surpasses the somewhat lackadaisical attitude of too many of their fellow students and other members of society. A sound and consistent work ethic is critical to succeeding. A lesson that must be taught by parents, with the wholehearted support of the academic system at all levels. Before the one world advocates considers this a slur on those who may not have yet gained citizenship, allow me a moment of clarification. Regardless of the legitimacy of any person's claim to citizenship or lack of verifiable documentation of same, I still hold to certain moral and ethical treatment owed all who enter our country. I have strong opinions on the recent spate of controversy regarding the growing, seemingly uncontrolled infusion of undocumented individuals. Yet, we must recognize the entry of thousands of individuals, whether illegally over the border of through the mass influx allowance of migrants fleeing the conflicts elsewhere, will create increasing economic, political and social difficulties. Again, let us leave such vocalization to others, many of whom are as ineffectual as me in correcting the problem.

As mentioned earlier, thousands of books are written yearly, espousing personal viewpoints on everything from unique diets to sexual antithesis. None bear any imprimatur other than being exactly what they should all declare in the forward – "This is my personal opinion or facts as I personally interpret them and it is very possible I don't have a single clue about the subject contained therein." So without further ado, this suggestion too joins that lemming's trek to the cliffs of implausibility.

What amazes me about the excess of such periodicals, is the number of out of date magazines I find in dentist's and doctor's offices. Why do so many of the publications seem to deal in golf or yachting or high powered automobiles or vacationing in exotic locations we might be able to visit were it not for the bill for services we will receive for our visits to their offices? Does anyone consider this a hint as to why our medical care costs seem to increase yearly? I've never seen a discount coupon pamphlet. Or how to save your money publication in any of those offices. I suppose that would be like finding a manual on refrigerator repair in the Antarctic.

And In the Beginning – As it were.

As to my genealogy, being adopted at the age of six, becoming an only child, I have no experience with siblings. Which of course lessens attendance at required holiday gatherings or funerals and limits the internecine quibbling when reviewing wills and possible inheritance shares. The major acceptance of biological relatives, however acquired, is their constituent function in continuing either the good or the bad of dynastic malfunction. In my case, being the bastard child at each familial gathering, those members of the extended family, on both of my adopted parent's side, were as tolerant of my attendance as their cultural prejudice would allow. But at times, trying to ingratiate myself with them, I felt as comfortable as wearing a yarmulke at a mosque.

My favorite literary line is from the novel, "Scaramouche," by Raphael Sabatini. Here he describes the essence of his hero saying, "He was born with a gift of laughter and a sense that the world was mad and that he was its progeny." If my gravestone would have the sufficient space, I would prefer that message be my epitaph. Humor has always been both a devotion of mine and a tool I've used to enter into social and professional groups in an anecdotal manner. Loneliness might have been a source of brief worry when I was much younger. Now, it is this innate solitude that surrounds my declining years and brings a delicious comfort.

I also have very strong views on the subject of adoption, to further expand on my wide divergence in opinion. The rational definition of adoption itself is to mean acceptance of one or more individuals from another non-biologically connected source. Missing is always the assurance of the ability to adapt on the part of the accepted and the acceptor. I was adopted by two amazingly wonderful people, who reflected the humanity and patience to take me from one strange world into their particular comfort zone. When one has become the refuse of disposable humanity, it must be recognized that the embrace of society is more tenuous, if not often difficult. The current brouhaha over the adoption by same sex married couples should never override the need for any child to have caring and involved parenting.

Birth is the result of a physical coupling between two humans, unless decided in the laboratory by the genetic futurists. Most often however, it is supposed, to engender thoughts of emotional connection. In my case, the birth mother was merely a vessel for instant gratification with no regard for my future status. She immediately left me to the warrants and care of others only two days after my birth. My birth father had no greater concern, even denying my existence, which required my removal from his doorstep where my biological, paternal grandfather, had delivered me, and from there to a nearby infant's hospital, courtesy of the local police. He contended not being able to understand why this strange bundle was left at his residence. Ironic that born on December 22nd, I appeared at his door, not of my doing or decision, on December 24th. I've always wondered if this entire undertaking was merely part of some unique Christmas gift exchange program. My entire conception process was about as emotional an experience as two petri dishes accidentally bumping into one another on a laboratory table.

It was this diffusion of parental lacking that has strengthened my objection to current judicial views of biology as a primary legal value in child custody cases. I've often been asked as to why I never wanted to seek contact with my biological progenitors. Very simple - why should I waste my good time to intrude into the lives of those for whom I would have been, at most, a momentary disruption and brief inconvenience? As to any biological siblings that still might be wandering around, I have enough trouble dealing with people I don't like, much less those with whom I have the barest genetic connection. Perhaps this is why I abhor the continual pandering of social service officials and child court judiciary, to the mammon of biological affinity and its supposed inviolable rule of law. Birth is a simple reaction of the female as a result of insemination of the male sperm to initiate the gestation period. See, I told my teacher I was awake and paying attention during that discussion in our high school biology class. Thus when that basic function is finished, the heretofore alien occupant is emitted into a world of which he or she had no awareness of or perhaps any original intent to join.

Too often we have excessively publicized the supposed sad, ill guided lives of celebrities who find adoption of children from other lands as absolving them of their apparent personal insufficiencies. I've never quite understood the need for Hollywood notables to engage in adoption crusades, knowing their newly acquired, fabricated family, will merely be left to the care of nannies and other household help while they continue to pursue even more public acclaim. It is narcissism at its height, possibly creating generations of singularly confused products of this rush to see who can adopt the most children of varied ethnic genetics. Surely there are other hobbies or charities to undertake that will have less potentially damaging ramifications. And not to be omitted, what of the thousands of children in our country needing the care and attention of newly acquired parents, many of them also of various ethnic identities if that be the desire of the adoption petitioner.

The laws regarding adoption are archaic and badly managed nationwide. More regrettably, they are poorly developed by buffoons in legislative chambers and administered by judicial juxtaposition who seem to have no understanding of a child's actual needs. As a member of a state mandated child services citizen review board a few years ago I was continually dismayed by the constant attribution of right of control to "birth parents". Adult begetters who were either relapsing from a multitude of rehabilitation attempts for alcohol and/or drugs, incarcerated for various felonies or were still engaged in activities considered within the most charitable of interpretations, as criminal. The children in question were too often denied a saner and more reasonable acceptance by couples who desired to become loving parents through adoption, gladly accepting any flaws in the child physically or emotionally. Biology is a science, not a legal precedent to be observed with rigidity. If current laws protect and demand these misguided biological mandates, then change the laws.

What has confused me most, is how one becomes a celebrity or a star in the vernacular of modern interpretation. After reading the backgrounds of so many of today's entertainment personages, I recognized my beginning was insufficient to merit any such accolades. My artistic talent ranged from less than mediocre and lacks any further mention. As for sports, say basketball, I had the dexterity of an elephant in a ballet class. My golfing ability could best be described by a good friend who was the professional at a nearby country club. While he was watching my efforts during an outing, I asked how I could improve my game. His response, "Take up chess - any sedentary activity." Enough of me for the moment, on to the next observation.

Are the Barbarians Coming Over the Wall?

I mentioned the need to respect the rights of every individual, whether here properly or by less than authorized means. However, today we are faced with the most pronounced invasion since the infamous wood beetle in our pristine forests. Illegal immigrants – or to be more politically correct, undocumented aliens who sneak across the border in droves or are brought here by criminal elements. To worsen the situation, individuals, after committing a crime, can flee back across the border where corrupt Mexican or other Latin American authorities refuse or fail to honor extradition treaties. These neighboring authorities allow their criminal elements to fire upon US Border Patrol agents and then move back into the safety of a government, which at its core, is a threat to our national security. Suggestion, a few of those Cobra gunships that have been returned to our control and not left by fleeing Iraqi military to the ISIS militants. With their sighting equipment and our skilled airmen, I have no doubt such assaults would lessen quickly. It could sure increase effective marksmanship training for our personnel. However, it is an extreme option that would bring out the ACLU's immediate response – as if they needed a reason to file a lawsuit.

Another of my uninformed and expressly conservative suggestions. Cite the judiciary that allows protection of those attempting to thwart this vigilance, and too often by violent means, for violation of their oath – "28 U.S Code 453. That reference is for those who have not been infected by the virus of lets hate America so prevalent in many supposed institutions of higher learning. To the multitude of the Hollywood effete, the misguided millennials and the stalwart tree huggers, the important part reads, ". . . and that I will faithfully and impartially discharge and perform all the duties incumbent upon me under the Constitution and laws of the United States. So help me God."

One can't be totally immune to the suffering and economic degradation many of these entrants have endured in their homelands. To seek a better life for oneself and one's offspring is a natural impulse. What is needed is for the five hundred and thirty five members of the institute for inefficiency, better known as Congress, to create, through an orderly and legal process, an acceptable criterion for those who truly deserve residency in this great country. But, once more, my voice is unheard against the howling wind of the inactive legislator.

To combat what the liberal factions referred to as an inhospitable and outrageous reference to Constitutional requirements, a new layer of ultra-liberal lunacy has been created – "sanctuary cities." Urban areas governed by those protected behind high fences or within exclusive, no minority allowed conclaves. That doesn't stop them from taking the tax money provided by the other law observing people elsewhere. Which proves my personal belief that the good people avoid political campaigning like measles or poison ivy, while the self-delusional become candidates and get elected by the unwary, too busy trying to survive in these chaotic times.

The former Obama administration filed a lawsuit against the state of Arizona regarding an immigration law, passed earlier by the state and that apparently certain parts had been ruled invalid by a Clinton appointed Judge. I suppose Mr. Obama, touted as a former instructor in constitutional law, has read the 10th Amendment to that same U.S. Constitution. And in the event he or the U.S. Attorney General, or others in the Justice Dept., had forgotten. Here it is. "Article 10 – The powers not delegated to the United States by the Constitution, nor prohibited by it to the States, are reserved to the States respectively, or to the people." Even to all those Harvard produced members of the High Court, can this be any clearer?

My military days, once so much impressed on my mind, its imagery never to be forgotten, has faded. Time spent in a National Guard unit and later an active duty stint for two years, for a time in Europe, as part of the then occupation forces in the early 1950's, provided little knowledge of what those who faced combat had endured. It did, however, imbue me with an appreciation for a reasonably disciplined rule of order. I did see firsthand, many of the destroyed portions of villages and cities as a result of the terrific horror of WW II. That period of military service would, however, later help me meet the demands of many activities I undertook. Vince Lombardi, famed coach of the NFL Green Bay Packers once said, "Discipline is when the boss says sit down and you don't even look for a chair."

Those who bore the brunt of pain and terror and anguish of battle, will forever have my deepest appreciation and concern for their welfare. Please note, since Roosevelt controlled the White House, only two presidents have had no military experience – both Democrats. One, using an Oxford scholarship to avoid his military obligation, and the other, too young when the draft ended in 1973. Of course, had the latter been eligible, he could have used one of his many contentions of being a foreign student that aided him so much in acquiring prestige educational access.

Since our former President, or his lackeys, appeared totally unaware of the needs of the veteran, part of the much vaunted stimulus package, instead of being used in the main to bail out the undeserving, should have been directed toward our military. To provide them reasonable separation bonuses, employment advocacy, medical and emotional care, as needed. Educational opportunities to enable them to reenter society and the job market on a level playing field. Recognize that PTSD or Post Traumatic Stress Disorder, although probably not recognized as such much earlier, has been with us since the first battle was fought for this country's beginning in 1775. The fog of war too often follows a military veteran through the rest of his or her life.

We must demand of our President and Congress that all Veteran Administration facilities, hospitals and personnel, be required to provide the best of care for those who stood and served at the wall. And immediately discharge all those administrators or other employees whose lack of interest, insufficiency in attention, or overt disregard, has brought such a pall of distrust over that organization. If ever accused of insufficient or improper behavior or lack thereof, the accused is placed on "paid leave" while a never ending – or as a matter of fact, never started hearing – conducted merely to acquiesce to the ever present Federal employees union influence. A more simple process. When misdeed or inappropriate action is found and verified – fire the bastard! No severance and no extension of benefits. Enough said.

We owe so much to these men and women, the children and grandchildren of the "Greatest Generation," and those who suffered the bitter Korean topography, the endless battles in the jungle stench of Vietnam and the current disaster in the deserts of the Mideast. I enjoy veteran's benefits and I am continually amazed when visiting the local VA hospital here in Salt Lake City, at the endurance and ability to survive by those many fellow veterans we know experienced the tension and stress of battle. To see the aging veterans of past battles, being very aware of their physical disabilities and health problems that may possibly lead to premature death, is sobering to any viewer. It could truly be said, "It may be God's waiting room." We in the Utah VA area enjoy tremendously dedicated and skilled medical services. But as with many government controlled institutions, the administrative sufficiency tends to fall below expectation and effectiveness.

Regrettably, there are VA institutions that have finally been spotlighted for gross inadequacy and outright fraudulent use of federal funds and services. But these same people are protected by that same egregiously controlled employee union contract. They suffered little if any punishment, and meanwhile they avoid discipline and their clients continue to suffer from their mishandling. With their unremitting forgetfulness, those in legislative power tarnish the memory of those who gave so much.

While my memory of matters and events, rather sharp, only a few decades ago, are now becoming more indistinct, I find myself roaming corridors ever farther back in the repository of my past. Here, in the evening of my existence, I find time has proven that the family remains the cornerstone of our modern civilization. The threat its status undergoes constantly in the liberal media, glorified reality films and the excessive adoration of celebrities, has weakened public perception as to the value of familial strength. It was Clarence Darrow, renowned attorney and personal rights activist, who once said, "The first half of our lives is ruined by our parents, and the second half by our children." For myself I have two serious concerns – first, that I can avoid my offspring needing to care for me as I age and my health were to fail. Secondly, to have the financial ability to care for my wife and myself. I never want her to be in need. Still, I personally don't want to be relegated to the waste heap of insignificance as a member of the human race or my localized society.

Opiate of the People or an Option for Hope?

Before I begin getting hate mail from everyone in the religious world, including the many self-ordained wearers of clerical garb and the assumed stature of prophet, let me preface the remarks herein. I don't disagree with anyone's right or reasoning in selecting and immersing themselves in any particular religious doctrine. I felt it important to cover this subject with greater personal emphasis than others herein. Man by his natural constitution, has always had an historic need to be subservient to some greater, heretofore unknown divine intercession. Mankind is a religious animal. Religion, whatever the form, and to whom the devotion and pleas are extended among the current selection of Gods, has for millenniums, formed the humanistic nature of most societies. I don't contend religion is bad, per se. It is however, as are all ideologies and doctrines, susceptible to mishandling, misinterpretations and abuse by those who have the ability to mislead faithful adherents to any theology or persuasion. My opinion and apologies to any clergy or religious hierarchy who may feel maligned. It is here, humbly offered.

We have been informed by those with a predilection for such minutia, that the percentage of those stating they are religious, in varying tones, has dropped markedly over the past decade or so. That the agnostic and atheist have gained a stronger foothold in the never ending emotional struggle among those who believe, those who don't and those who personally care little about the subject. Of course, that again, is the basis of individual freedom to choose. I just don't want the ultra-doctrinal oriented to preach in the street and block up the traffic too often. And for those who don't believe in anything, leave the religious types alone and go off and play in that same traffic I don't want blocked.

The Jewish people, with their ages of rigid orthodoxy, have suffered centuries of oppression wherever they lived. Often they were the stable basis of commerce and social advancement of the societies into which they had melded. The pogroms of Czarist Russia, the vicious campaign of Hitler to erase them from the face of the earth, and the later purges of the Stalin era that blemished that country's amazing history beyond many other global communities, are milestones in the Judaic history. Still today, the Jew must endure prejudice and governmentally inflicted bias in many parts of the globe. Dealing with past atrocities, they suffered as a people and a culture, hopefully declining, nevertheless, there has for centuries been present in the Qur'an of Mohammed, dictates that threatens Judaism's very existence. Could it be to merely elevate Islam's own misconstrued desire for self-importance and dominance, or to shadow their own theological inadequacy?

Roman Catholic history has been stained by venality of the inquisition during the middle Ages and more recently the hideous specter of child molestation, still unresolved by "Holy Mother the Church." This allowance or lack of oversight regarding such an abomination, lies at the feet of the head of the church – and that is the Pope. Only he can bring the hammer down and require all such incidents be immediately reported to local law enforcement for the necessary investigation, and where warranted, the most severe prosecution.

The very recent entry by the current papal head, Pope Francis, into the arena of political pronouncement, has added another potential point of immediate criticism. Some opponents are not assured they need a former aggressive, Argentinian activist, wearing the supreme MITRE. They merely want the Vatican to continue its aura of traditional vapidity. His interference into the ongoing Palestinian state imbroglio, and comments on the global warming issue, or internal American issues, creates a false sense that the Vatican is more than the illusionary country, created centuries ago to merely protect its security from invading hordes. Now he is a champion of those arguing income inequality and the ongoing dispute over the climate change controversy. His desire to be a global voice has even extended to commentary relative to the winner of the 2016 Presidential election. Although viewed by millions as having an international persona, he does not represent everyone. Also, I am again in a quandary as to the increasing number of sainthood proposals being proffered. If this continues, I may need to invest in one of those companies who design and manufacture all those little commemorative medals.

Last but not least, the ravings of radical Islamic Mullahs and Imams, who preach a form of religious idolatry, emphasized with the Qur'an in one hand and a bloody sword in the other. Just a brief statement of addition to the primary list, but I will have more to say later Just a quick note. There exist twisted claimants, too often, Imams & Mullahs, justifying certain of Mohammed's teachings, continually supporting terrorism in the name of jihad and its misinterpreted Quranic doctrine. Attempting to infiltrate our country with newly radicalized mental miscreants to create domestic terrorism. A comic recently remarked, "The way to distinguish a toddler from a terrorist at an airport security gate? The terrorist wears the diaper on his head.

And from these three trees of original monotheism, grew the forest of most theological dictatorships we endure today. To many, the close involvement in any religious gathering is a warm embrace to protect and comfort them in a world, which in their estimation, reels in dizzying spirals from conflict to conflict. It is the biblical "Balm of Gilead." If it provides at least a modicum of comfort, I support their devotion to the theology of choice. So long as its basic tenets do not proscribe any adverse action toward other religious affiliations, or would force me to support their actions or demands that may limit my Constitutional rights and freedom to think as I will.

If however, to the faithful adherent, it is their hallucinogen of choice, it can, quickly, become an ongoing opportunity to lose themselves in a mist of fantasy that too often hides the real world. Rather, could they not deal with the needs of the time and use the tenets of their faith to adjust theirs, and others', approaches to critical situations. There is always a cruel side to blind faith – an increasing naiveté that often foretells abuse of the adherents and excess of power wielded by its leadership. Such exaggerated zealotry raises the banner of religious faith as a martial escutcheon. Their beliefs become a weapon to force others to accede to their particular view of right and wrong, privilege and prohibition. And of course, to increase the coffers of offerings and donations that enriches the spellbinder, the haranguer – the newly espoused prophet.

There are those who would, if pressed, profess being Christians, but do not shout it from the rooftop or demand their particular beliefs be the basis for every decision made by they or others. Jews, who bear the traditions of four thousand years, silently honor their forefathers, often with little desire for discordant outcries as is the hallmark of many evangelical spokes persons. There are many Muslims who practice the peace and emotional quietude as spoken of eloquently in certain parts of the Qur'an. But regrettably certain sections, or "suras", in that same book, speak strongly to the need to destroy the unbeliever. To take up arms and deny others of their right to believe as they would. The radical element has debased their faith by fictionalizing those earlier censures and creating the schism between them and non-adherents of Islam.

It's difficult for me to answer the age old question, "Is there actually a heaven or hell?" How should I know? Never been there, unless you count Saturday night in Leesville, LA, when I was there during my early time in the Army. Of course, if there's no hell, a lot of evangelical preachers are obtaining money under false pretenses. I really don't wish to spend my remaining years being in fear of the consequences were I to be found, by some higher authority, to merit the better or warrant the worse. Now that I've expressed my undying loyalty to the Constitutional protection of individual rights in this area, let us journey further down the path into darker caverns of thought. Thus, where is the problem? The differing philosophical origins that have caused centuries of chaos, brutality and misery, much for unknown reasons, still seems to separate people from their common roots?

John Lennon of the renowned Beatles musical group, may have been somewhat misquoted years ago by a muddled media, when he was supposed to have said, "We," meaning the Beatles, "may be more popular than Jesus Christ." Yet in fact, his full comment may have merely been a lament that in today's very materialistic society, their youthful fans too often placed their adoration of pop music over that of a belief in a divine being. The remark, of course, was immediately misinterpreted by a tabloid oriented press.

And there's the feminine appearing, beaux arts eye glasses wearing, Elton John, idol of the modern music genre, who more recently declared his opinion that religion should be banished? Even more recently reportedly saying, Jesus was gay and that religion is harmful to the human psyche. Now, Mr. John enjoys the freedom of speech granted residents of the United States, although he is one of the numerous human foibles the English people have foisted upon us. His views are as shallow as his lifestyle, and possibly only acceptable to those without more than a passing concept of what it entails to live in a world of varying, and often divergent beliefs. Then again, his views on Jesus could merit him a place as Grand Marshal in the next LGBT parade.

Religious adherence is the necessary heartbeat for many. During modern times, certain Hollywood celebrities have embraced the charlatan doctrine of former, meagerly read, science fiction author, L. Ron Hubbard. Their very espousal of Scientology has merely added another name to the long list of pseudo contemplative, spiritual revelations. An ersatz theology that will keep its adherents in close communication as long as their checkbooks continue to fund this mendacious misleading of the Hollywood elite. An increasing number of new religious doctrines appear more designed for fleecing the unwary and gullible, than the fluorescing of true self divination and recognition.

Yet, it must be understood that total control of its believers has always been the mainstay of all religions. Without it, domination becomes impossible. And without this absolute control, the architects of these religious outpourings are unable to deal with the natural free spirit born in each of us. The numerous examples of cults and other synthetic religious fostering's, have too often ended in tragic results for its benighted membership. The doings of these psychopathic rejects is too bothersome to relate here; Jim Jones, psychotic prophet of the poor who led over 900 to their deaths in the steaming jungle of Guinea. David Koresh, the self-proclaimed messiah who forced an ill-staged conflict in Waco, Texas, losing the life of dozens, many being children.

Any religion, however simple in its approach or basic doctrine, requires a great leap of faith and at times, certain aspects that seem to deny reality. And let us not, for more than a moment, ever forget the TV bamboozler, able to cry at a moment's notice, Jimmy Swaggart. The earlier couple devoted to the con, Jim & Tammy Baker and others who continue to fleece more of their faithful than an expert sheep shearer. The uniquely named Creflo' Dollar and his wife. Perhaps his mother lost her book of baby names. He and his wife are beginning to look more like Jim & Tammy. And not to forget the dispenser of "miracle water", for a price of course, Peter Popoff and TV's most evident booster of dental brilliance Joel Osteen. Dear reader, the hucksters of old have not disappeared. The shill artists and carny ballyhoo of the county fair midway are still with us on TV and in many pulpits.

So without extensive experience in understanding the major ideological writings, the Bible, The Torah, the Quran or the Book of Mormon, I've still never found any jocularity in any of these volumes. Attention, all you graduates of the eastern universities or the costal campuses of the misinformed, the word jocularity means humor. End of lesson. Of course, with all that foretelling of disaster, plagues of every imaginable nature, the vengeance of an angry God and in the case of the Qur'an, the need to violently rid themselves of non-believers, I doubt there would be much material for comedians to employ.

The Bible reportedly has 66 "books" in the Old Testament and 27 in the New Testament. Inasmuch as I have not read all of them or various interpretations of the initial versions, I leave their meaning, authenticity and authorship to those with more time and academic time on their hands. The Torah is bulging with prohibitions, instructions to maintaining religious exactness and many philosophical utterances. The Qur'an, a mass of suras' or chapters cover the sayings of a former camel dealer, ostensibly transcribed by his devoted followers over fourteen centuries ago. The Book of Mormon relates episodic history of America that reads as a convolution of fact and religious fervor. Thus, it is up to the reader of any of them, as to deciding what a factual occurrence was and what falls between the documented and the doctrinal, strictly your choice. Regrettably, too many are influenced by the charlatans of confusion as they pronounce without fact, and declare a wisdom and foresight, impossible to the human species. I really don't have the time to conjecture what is to be believed by the faithful, regardless of the paucity of truth.

Ancient peoples fought over control of land or perceived slurs. The plethora of Gods available was the choice of many individual nations and societies. They seemed to understand the need to divorce themselves from the particular dogma of other non-related ethnic or cultural entities. The overpowering mysticism and magical composition of belief in any deity or group therein, caused all to be hesitant and reluctant to challenge even the captured enemy, their individual religious proclivities. They ignored the Gods of others for fear they themselves might earn the wrath of some deity they neither knew nor understood.

To a Scene More Local

Because the history of the Catholic Church has been so academically reviewed, publicized and criticized over the centuries, I thought it interesting to now reflect more closely on a unique religious competitor with the other three. The Mormons, more formally The Church of Jesus Christ of Latter Day Saints, "LDS," is headquartered in Salt Lake City, Utah, where I currently dwell. So let us begin there. With an ever expanding growth, particularly abroad through its massive missionary effort, it too was highly criticized and faced adversity in its earlier existence. Some of that animosity, socially and politically, still exists today. This original theological precept was ostensibly first expressed by their 19th Century, self-ascribed prophet, Joseph Smith. The LDS, for all its family values preeminence and declarations of equality among all mankind, did relegate female members into more subservient positions. It should be noted though, it was the State of Utah that first gave females the right to vote, a right, which unfortunately, was delayed by the rest of the nation for years.

The Book of Mormon, to its critics, is considered an extensive work of fiction, encompassing Smith's original and much disputed contentions. To its faithful, it was an absolute guide that most of its members equate with the Torah, New Testament and the Qur'an, although lately cracks have appeared in that former, formidable wall of theological structure. This alone, in the opinion of numerous self-deigned biblical scholars, is in contradiction to present authoritative history. It is claimed by some, the Book of Mormon is merely the attempt of an unlettered farm boy, to take advantage of the frenetic cavalcade of religious revivalists dominating the rural scene in the 1820s. Not having lived during Smith's era, and not being a religious scholar, who am I to say his visions were not just the mental imagery of an overly impressionable youth? Or possibly, revelation from a higher power and has the substance its adherents believe is the word of God, as dictated to this, Joseph Smith, by whatever ethereal force might exist.

Archaeologists, historians, paleontologists and various geo-science experts, have expressed serious doubts about or have never found any tangible evidence of the fictional groups, contended to be ancient ancestors of today's LDS heirs, as purported in the Book of Mormon. The substance of which was supposedly, derived from 'golden plates," found near Palmyra, New York by the young Smith. The religion's preeminent position within the state of Utah reflects itself in the near total domination of the legislative, judicial and local municipal governance in over one hundred and seventy years since its predecessors first entered into the valley of the Great Salt Lake. Although instrumental in the development of the area, and its ensuing success as a highly successful part of the Intermountain region, their rather austere social prohibitions still mark them as ultra-conservative by the more liberal element.

One similarity common to the three declared prophets of the past, has long perplexed me. Referring to Jesus Christ, Muhammed and to a marked degree, Joseph Smith, history doesn't indicate any writings by their personal hand. Rather, everything they supposedly said, or sacred teachings preached, were then transcribed by others or recalled in later versions by their followers. Jesus spoke from a mountain top. Mohammed sat reflecting and having his utterances recorded by others. Joseph Smith was said to have peered into a hat, holding a "seer stone," to reveal the secrets of the fabled golden plates he asserted was the basis of his revelations. The results, reportedly recorded by another person.

The major blemish on the LDS remarkable journey and development of the now fertile Salt Lake Valley, was the ugliness of polygamy. Banished from legitimate church doctrine well over one hundred and twenty years ago, it still exists in small individual enclaves, again casting a degree of censure, however marginal, on the mainstream Church. Polygamy, regardless of its proponents claim to its biblical heritage, is repugnant to society as a whole. It creates a method of literally forcing young girls into a life of subservience and obeisance to men far older than they. It is simply a form of pseudo sexual molestation. Regardless, local and state law enforcement in both southwest Utah and portions of northeast Arizona, just across the border, where the FLDS, the polygamous outcasts from the church, the *"Fundamentalist Latter Day Saints,"* allow them to function seemingly unimpeded. At best, they appear laggard in prosecuting those who openly violate the laws pertaining thereto. Lack of both state and the federal oversight and action, is directly responsible for this egregious situation to flourish as a continuing embarrassment to two beautiful states.

Today, the LDS's former strict condemnation of both same sex marriage and homosexuality itself, has been tempered through evolving thought and consideration within the church's administration, coupled with the politically correct rise in national conscience. However, recent declaration by that same authority, prohibits children of same sex marriage receiving the "blessings of the church." Supposedly, when reaching adulthood, they must disavow their male or female parents in order to receive acceptance by the hierarchy of the church. Yet, in the 2015 Salt Lake City mayoralty election, the winner was a lesbian. "Three members of the city council are announced gay, and a transgender was a candidate in one of the area's lesser election campaigns. Like the famed Dylan lyric, "Times, they are a changing."

Nevertheless, one aspect of the Mormon faith has long bothered me. I was raised Catholic, and although no longer a faithful attendee at mass, I would still be welcome if I wished to stop in to any of their religious gathering. Although not a practicing Jew, I could walk into a synagogue, hopefully acquiring a yarmulke to show my respect, and be well greeted. Also, I could enter a Mosque, removing my shoes in obeisance to the appropriate protocol and respect. Many years ago I visited a Buddhist house of prayer and was warmly greeted.

Yet, even many of the LDS members can't enter any of their temples without first having acquired a "temple recommend." A strange process, wherein they must obtain from their local "bishop", this recognition of their being a faithful and tithing person in good standing in the church. Family members of a couple being married within one of these temples must be accepted in this form so as to be able to actually attend their child or relative or friend's wedding, or they will be prohibited entry for the ceremony. The hypocrisy of this prohibition rankles many and casts doubts on the supposed open spirit so often proclaimed by the LDS and its thousands of missionaries trotting the globe.

So there, now I've really stepped into it. First, those with similar religious proclivities will denounce me as a bigot; possibly, a heretic. The American Civil Liberties Union, *the ACLU,* may pounce on me for demeaning religious freedom. And ethicists will contend such is none of my business to contest. But then, this is the same ACLU that openly defended the right of swastika bearing, white Aryan thug groups, to parade through Skokie, IL, home of so many Holocaust survivors. And later they were in the front lines when they came to the aid of that polemic embarrassment to education, Ward Churchill, formerly on the faculty of the U. of Colorado, where he spewed anti-Holocaust and anti-American instruction to young minds, still disengaged from reality by their numbing adherence to such verbal vagabonds.

Regardless of all this commentary, even today, the scent of incense and the Latin liturgy of the traditional Catholic mass, now rarely practiced, harkens me back to my youth as an altar boy. I still remember my beloved mother's comment when we attended mass together during a visit home from college. The declared, modern non-Latin liturgy was imposed in many churches. A young seminarian was sitting on the step leading up to the altar, strumming a guitar, attempting to render some type of newer pop music hymn. On the way home my mother quipped, "Our regular mass has turned into Sing along with Mitch," referring to the then popular song oriented TV favorite, Mitch Miller and his ensemble of voices.

The historicity of Catholicism's errors, both social and economic, will quickly reveal its many diversions and questionable periods. The more recent revelations regarding child and youth molestation, and the pedophile culture among certain segments of its clergy, has regrettably haunted the church for the past century and severely stained the credibility of its leadership. The middle Ages saw the persecution of the Jews and the horrendously vicious institution of the Inquisition. The abuses which many historians contend, led directly to the Great Protestant Reformation of the early 16th Century, urged by such religious protagonists as Martin Luther and the eventual schism with the Catholic Church. The current Catholic Pontiff, a former pro-Peronist activist in Argentina's fitful political and economic conflicts, rules by selective fiat, and not by election by the people that encompass his constituency – the faithful adherents.

The mainstream sects, Methodists, Episcopalian, Lutheran, Baptist, Protestants, etc., have in most instances walked the middle road on many issues facing an ever diverse society. They have, when group pressure required, decried the more radical and less palatable doctrine espoused by the extreme evangelical right. Disappointedly, an ever burgeoning evangelical movement often hides an overly emotional outpouring of its adherents' advocacy, declaring their leadership as "charismatic." Further, these present day diviners generate millions in revenue from those attending in person and through the intrusive influence of the TV medium. Architecturally grotesque places of worship are built, emulating the great edifices of the middle Ages. The sufficiently funded evangelical right has now enmeshed itself in a political process that is supposed to be free of such unrelated influences.

I list these many variations simply as examples of how religion can be perverted to fit personal agendas, and to reap profits never considered a doctrine of the truly faithful. Today, we have some of that former, ancient idol worship mimicry by a few of the modern religious icons. In this writer's conservative opinion, such abuse by these ersatz modern prophets, insults the reality of traditional religious belief. My major objection concerning any of the religious ideologies is the often crushing burden of complete subservience by the devoted follower. A demand that will quickly extinguish the light of personal choice and creative liberty.

Before concluding this myriad of non-academic and strictly personal viewpoints, please allow one last individual assumption. Regardless of those who are want to relate Islam as a horrific chapter in the development of religion, we must be aware; Islam was the source of some of the most innovative mechanical and engineering feats in the history of mankind. Its contribution to the arts and architecture has been unparalleled throughout the ages. The Jewish culture, long been criticized for their propensity to develop financial institutions, however, are also responsible for developing monetary systems still the hallmark of our modern economic foundation.

Now that I have thoroughly offended all whose religious leanings and organization mentioned, let me state my personal position on this subject. I've come to accept that if mankind didn't have individual Gods to believe in, their vision of a personal tomorrow would leave them constantly peering into an unfathomable abyss. Furthermore, many adherents to the principal religious orthodoxies are not diametrically opposed to other viewpoints, or overly obsessive in their particular belief. It is this rational and fair appraisal of the differences that are part of a diverse society. In our country, freedom to practice your religion of choice is a sacrosanct mandate in the Constitution – a freedom that must not be hindered, impeded or curbed by any external or liberal effort.

However, in doubtful deference to the unbeliever, agnostic or avowed atheist, that group that insists any type of declared or imagined divine intervention is merely hallucinatory imagining, I also insist on providing fair hearings and equality of position in society. Theirs is a heady comment for just saying, they don't believe in any God or non-real presence by any other than those on the scene of any event or action – right? But still it is a well ensconced opinion held by many. So to accept their side – just for the sake of a trying to be fair and what they may consider incredulous, we can quickly glance back at what has been written factually and fictionally over the past several mileniums.

Abraham, reputed patriarchal head of what would become the Jewish nation and eventually the State of Israel. According to ancient scripture, accepted what he felt was the will of God to sacrifice his young son after sending off another one into the barren desert. And not to forget the biblical figure – Moses – who parted seas and brought down from a mountain the inscribed law supposedly provided by what, according to scripture, he assumed was God. A set of rules forming the moral code for millions thereafter, while ignored by many others. Of course one cannot avoid mention of the itinerant carpenter, whose recorded life by numerous writers formed the primer for the evolution of Christianity, its massive growth and the ever present visage of a papal authority unquestioned by millions of its followers. Six centuries later a camel trader marries a wealthy widow, and once removed from mundane labor, sits himself down to murmur philosophies and doctrinal teachings that soon formed the Islamic era.

Of course there arrived many years later the reformist, Martin Luther, upset the theological apple cart with his protestation leading to the formation of dozens of religious sects that dominate the lesser acknowledged sphere of denominational numbers. A myriad of various dogmas that shouted forth vocal rants of street preachers to the gatherings in ragged tents in muddy fields. Finally to the cavernous cathedrals of the later ages, and now to today's grotesque structures, supposedly emulating past monumental religious structures, further enhanced by television and radio. The reinterpretation of religions position in the matrix of an emerging future will continue. It has been a part of human evolution for thousands of years – and will undoubtedly remain.

There I've linguistically stepped into it. I've probably insulted the beliefs of more than a few billion – so be it. I felt the need to cross over and shed some light on the probable disagreement many have with organized adherence to a divinity, mankind has argued about, fought over, tragically slew wantonly to either expand or decimate, but may never have actually seen. It remains the most sensitive and conflict generating subject in the history of mankind. Yet, if the reader demands fairness, and equally opinion, what is written here merely fulfills that demand.

What is aging – really?

I've spent over forty-five years of my life involved in entertainment/sports and exhibition facility management, major league sports operations and a number of international sports events. Now that doesn't make me automatically qualified above all other candidates seeking any particular position, but it's the statistics of my employment search the few years, after completing my stay with the 2002 Winter Olympic Games organization, that blatantly displayed the control of the particular dominant church here in Utah. I submitted over a hundred resumes for positions that I felt I had at least the basic qualifications to fulfill or receive an interview of interest. As a result, I a number of postcard like responses that they'd already filled the position or my credentials did not warrant further interest. The other half of inquiries, and resumes submitted, apparently never warranted a reply. Of the remaining number, interviews were achieved for perhaps ten or so job openings.

During these face to face meetings with potential employers, I was asked a particular line of questions. As an example, in what "ward" (an LDS congregation location), I resided? Did I know certain individuals in my residential area, all being ostensibly "bishops" in the church?" Or was my stay in Ohio, according to my resume, "part of my "mission," the interviewer not understanding I was born and raised there. For the uninitiated, all these terms or inquiries refer directly to membership in the Church of Jesus Christ of Latter Day Saints, LDS, or the more colloquial, Mormons. Almost immediately after my answer to the obverse, the interview was over. I was thanked, never hearing another word. I thought such discrimination was illegal, unless my failure to be hired was because I was too old or attended a university where drinking was never really frowned upon. Job searching is basically a tenuous activity everywhere, yet in Utah, regardless of the normal public calm and nearness of the beautiful mountains, the state retains a 19th Century mentality in a 21st Century age.

More Fuel on the Fire

During my tenure in major sports and entertainment facility management, a number of those years were spent during the Vietnam protest era. It was a difficult time for all concerned, operators of facilities, local governing authorities and law enforcement. We were faced with an onslaught of tirade of foul language, offensive behavior and at times violent reaction, all carried forth in the name of freedom of speech and demand for the end of, what the protestors contended, was an unjust military action overseas. Young people, the mainstay of such movements, felt they were a force for global justice and human rights. The problem with them and the current mob of millennials, demanding an even greater voice, in their constant whining and spouting unfathomable mouthing, most of them wouldn't know the difference between Karl Marx and Groucho Marx.

Sadly, many of them were merely modern day camp followers, more dedicated to the drink and drugs that was so prolific in such groups. They were euphoric in the belief they were on the right side, regardless of the less savory elements that too often impregnated the core of each movement. And further, exacerbating many such gatherings, was the mercurial and totally inane nature of many musical groups and entertainers during that period, merely using the mistaken enthusiasm of their followers to promote themselves. Their lack of true resonance with the anti-war effort gave lie to an attitude, more fiscal than factual.

During my career, I witnessed endless concert events where young people, so laced with unauthorized pharmaceuticals, were protesting a conflict in Asia they little understood. The number of arrests for drug use and dealing, weapons possession, drunkenness, and excessive displays of the human anatomy, grew exponentially as the Vietnam crisis continued. When the fighting in that far Asian clime ceased, many of the music artists found new objects or causes for their rants during their expensively ticketed events. Like saving the whales, the legalization of Marijuana and numerous similar trivial protestations becoming the norm. Yet today, we of the older end of society, are again nonplussed when viewing the current exaggerated trends in our youth's costuming and personal behavior. Only several decades ago, the leadership of our younger citizens was primarily in the hands of the then most current music phenomena – the increasingly bizarre and erratic acting, pop or "hard rock" personalities.

During that same period, however I had the privilege and pleasure of hosting concerts by such greats as, John Denver, Neil Diamond, Bruce Springsteen, the inimitable Harry Belafonte, Glenn Campbell, and the tremendously entertaining Beatles. And of course the reputed musical "King", Elvis

Presley. Never to forget the "moon walk" of the highly talented Michael Jackson and English phenomenon, Mick Jagger. Or performances by such masters of melody as the incomparable Johnny Mathis, the always exciting Dionne Warwick, the crowd pleasing nature of Lionel Ritchie and Aretha Franklin. There was the plethora of crowd pleasing "doo-wop," that melodic soiree into harmony that presaged much of today's so-called pop rock. Let us not omit the excitement generated by Johnny Cash and Kenny Rogers, Loretta Lynn, Dolly Parton and the many artists who moved effortlessly from pure country to the heights of the more urban sound... I regret there are so many other deserving artists to mention, but time and space again limit their inclusion. Theirs was a magic on stage that made the other less desirable imitations bearable, they were the heart of the industry.

Traveling Back for a Moment

Allow me to wander further afield to other places I have resided. Sioux Falls, South Dakota was an interesting start to my facility management career. It was a dot on most road maps and even less significant in the jargon of urban importance. It had a rather non inviting culture. In reality, unless boredom and social depression were categorized as a genetic trait, culture was not rampant. Any attempt by the adventuresome to engage I any active choice of life styles, either brought social rebuff or total absence of acknowledgement. It was though the land visited by the original settlers, would be a place becalmed from the movement of human progress and social change. As a local whit once remarked, "Now you know why General Custer went to fight at the "Little Big Horn; if you've ever spent a Saturday night in Sioux Falls". I once looked up the archaic expression "obtuse" and it directed me right to the city.

Memphis, Tennessee, during my earlier stay there, remained a stronghold of segregated minds, even with the loosening of previously denied public facilities. Sound minded people still mired in the fantasy of racial superiority. It was an urban expansion seeking a way out of the once confining sophistication demanded of a society, who held fast to the belief of their forebears. That race was a given factor of separation of peoples based on their skin color and earlier domain. Regardless of Supreme Court rulings and the new freedoms purported with the passage of the Civil Rights Act, it was still deep in the mental equation of the people to resist, however subtle or benign in approach and attitude. The immediate area, like many parts of the south, still fought to rid their past of the sludge of Democratic intransigency to needed change in personal views and too long held visions of a fading past.

St. Louis, MO was in constant worry over the close location of E. St. Louis, IL. A community where corruption, crime and racial imbalance, had so infected the city's governance as to make the site unwanted, socially and commercially. However, St. Louis, during my brief stay, seemed to retain a degree of urban exuberance and portends to become every year, the city its residents desire. It remains an interesting, and in my personal memory, a pleasant place to live. A sprawling populated area that was comprised of distinctly separate ethnic neighborhoods, where diversity was as marked and evident as its many architecturally varied structures. There one could find the genesis of soccer in America. A fact too little mentioned in the promotional output by the current Major League Soccer - MLS. I was privileged to be involved in one of the initial professional clubs there and without those many local amateur clubs fostering the sport over the years, I seriously believe there would not be the current rise of interest in the sport in our country.

Niagara Falls, NY was the epitome of political incest. I remember during the initial weeks of my stay, the then Mayor of the city spoke to a number of we recently employed, supervisory employees. He was reportedly a defrocked minister who proudly tooled his white Cadillac convertible around the city on constant tours and parades. He was quite emphatic that we all understood the basic principles of how matters were resolved and decisions affecting the local citizens occurred. Holding up three fingers, he impressed on we assembled new employees, that as long as any proposal had three votes of the five member city council, implementation of any submission would follow, regardless of its worth or merit or even the unethical nature of the measure involved.

As has occurred in the past, I was fortunate to encounter the friendship of several rather unique individuals. The first City Manager I worked for in Niagara Falls was a man of estimable integrity, who eventually saw fit to leave that corrupt political menagerie during my stay. A man, ill-suited to the puppetry required by the entrenched demagoguery that passed for local government. He was replaced by a subservient political lackey and municipal miscreant. Enough said, as the city was deserving of his incompetency and obvious lack of moral compass.

During this time I became acquainted with two, somewhat dissimilar, but trustworthy individuals, talented and dedicated to their assigned responsibilities. One was the city's Planning Director, who was Jewish. The other, a somewhat diminutive gentlemen of Arabic heritage, the new assistant city engineer. We, the Jew, the Arab and the strayed Catholic, were involved in elements of the construction of a new "International Convention Center." A facility intended to bring enrichment to a city whose lure as a tourist or visitor location was close to nil, except for the contiguous, famed Niagara Falls. We three would often have lunch together. When asked what we three *unlike types* would ever talk about. I merely replied that I would draw a line of water like a border on the table and let the other two argue over it. Loved that response to the questioners, who never understood the irony of the answer.

This design and construction of a major convention/arena structure in the downtown area allowed me to become associated with the facility's architects, the renowned Philip Johnson and his talented partner, John Burgee, whose offices were in New York City. To meet with Johnson, one of the 20th Century's most notable architectural innovators, was to truly accompany the shadow of a giant. My stay in that city by the `Falls' revealed to me that governmental venality, however cloaked, is a silent disease. It's never too obvious and always desirous to seek anonymity. Like the insidious cockroach, light will disclose their location and force them to scurry for cover. And again like the flat, dark brown beetle sized insect, without constant vigilance, such creatures will always return. Election by a poorly informed or inattentive constituency will constantly allow the reemergence of evil. A truism that has reached upward into the highest levels of national legislative power.

North Carolina, my next stop, was a state wrapped in the grandeur of its western mountains to the impressive roll of its wave lashed eastern coastline. A people deeply invested in the future with its major industries and futuristic research facilities. Yet still so tied to a fascinating past. Unlike a number of the surrounding states, North Carolinians remain more dedicated to bettering the lot of their own populace rather than living in the dying visage of a confederacy, long a subject for novels. It has been said, a people form the genetic seed of their own later, social crop. That in the end, their strength or inability to resist, will determine their capacity to survive the winter of discontent and the summer heat of inevitable change. But my travels continued.

The city of Dallas, TX, is a broad panorama with its restless environs, its desire to be more than standard Texan imagery. Where the massiveness of the landscape was too often overpowered by the exaggeration of its inhabitants, Dallas still reflected what is good, if not sometimes a caricature of western bravado. Humorous in some instances, its people still echo the resilience of the state's earliest intruders who fought Indians, the established Mexican government, who battled, and what to them, was an invasion by the upstart American "gringo." Coupled with a climate that could, and often did, test the mettle of man. Their heavy Hispanic heritage is a credit to their ability to succeed in so many ventures.

I cannot omit our tenure in New Orleans. A city famed for its unique cuisine and historic past. Yet, one still deep within the corrupt shell of an even more dissolute state government. New Orleans has always been on the cusp of a natural disaster. One must feel sorrow for those lives lost and terrible damage wreaked by hurricane `Katrina'. Yet, when we lived there, the vaunted levee and flood control system was under constant criticism by the many, and the meat of ongoing media expose. The construction, lack of upkeep and incompetence in its management, was a constant reminder of a major catastrophe, just a storm away. Despite its attempts to revive, it still remains a shabby glimpse of what could be.

And of course there were our two stays in Atlanta, GA, where the forces of population growth have created more division than diversity. It is a city that depends on its suburban extensions for survival, inasmuch as the central core has become too insecure. And like other large mega metropolises, the nature of downtown Atlanta continues to drive its best talent and potential residents away to a more secure and habitable periphery. It is dynamic in its varied amenities, but retains a government in its central core that continually fails its constituency.

This instant travelogue is now finished, presumably capped by the earlier recitation of my present abode in the Salt Lake City area.

Why the Law and Legality are never the same

I own numerous copies of the United States Constitution, and at least a dozen books that specifically address each Article and Amendment. Additionally, I covet my volumes on the lives and decisions of past Supreme Court Justices, Oliver Wendell Holmes, Roger B. Taney, Charles Evans Hughes, Earl Warren and Warren E. Burger. One also needs to be cognizant of the more modern interpreters in black robes; Associate Justices, William O. Douglas, Louis Brandeis, Benjamin Cardozo, Hugo Black, Thurgood Marshall, William Rehnquist, and on. Not for a moment forgetting the giant among plebian black robed colleagues, the recently deceased, Antonin Scalia. To this writer, since the three newest appointees have arrived, we may continually experience a dissident crew, now ensconced on the judicial dais, high above the petitioner's podium in that august structure.

So why my apparent obsession with this particular aspect of American legal system? Simply I love the Constitution for its diagrammatical proposition for freedoms, never before enjoyed by man. It is a fascinating work of individuals whose inbred prejudices and preformed concepts of man's place in the diorama of life, had to be re-forged. They were required to put aside century's long declarations of man's dominion over those they conquered or were considered less ennobled. We should never forget the anonymous comment made by another, far more erudite than I; "Our country, founded by imperfect men who formed a perfect union."

So lamentable that elimination of slavery and the subjection of women, to less than equal social, financial and political status, remained vacant in the initial writing. Its absence from the original Bill of Rights was changed only after internecine political battling and the tragedy of the Civil War. For all its often claimed flaws, I still view the Constitution as a beautifully crafted document, embodying the desires of a people, long oppressed by monarchial regimes. It is not, however, anymore the totally inclusive and reactive document initially desired. Our ancestors knew change would and must occur, thus the Amendment process. However, in the minds of certain specific causes, it must be altered constantly to reflect the needs of particular groups, when and how dominant the demands. It is this frenzy to change without the extended thought required that endangers the basic substance of the document.

We as a constituency of the freest form of government ever known to man, must purposely and with dedication, pursue the clarification of our constitutional rights. The buzz words of varying supposed progressive opinions, is the expression, "as interpreted." If misused, as has been bandied about by certain disproportionately liberal elements of our society, it could bring to an end that great dream – that singular light of freedom that has attracted so many to this land from throughout the globe for almost 240 years.

Supreme Court Associate Justice, Louis D. Brandeis, said in a 1928 talk, "The greatest danger to liberty lurks in the insidious encroachment of men of zeal, well-meaning but without understanding the consequences." It's critical that we recognize that imperfections may still reside within the substance of the Constitution, and like the apparent beauty of a visually acceptable subject, a closer examination can and will reveal flaws, however microscopic and at first, mere blemishes. The more modern liberal concept is to approach the Constitution as a mere scribbling of a few suggested guidelines. Some wish to see it forced to become easily variable and malleable, so as to meet the altering face of an increasingly polyglot populace. Yet, to change without great thought and extended review, is to move too fast, simply to just meet political and personal whims at the time.

Man has long disagreed about the eminence of law as a moral guideline.   Because the law is a product of man's personal consideration and desire, it can be the reflection of society at the time of its creation. To others, it is prejudice, formalized into a language. More often than not it is indistinguishable from personal viewpoint. The imagination of doing good can permeate legislatives thinking when creating laws. Many contend that lawmaking is an honorable method of undoing that which social ills have promulgated. Forgotten has been the true purpose of government; to protect its citizenry and safeguard them from intrusion by alien forces. Today's legislator is 90% politician, 5% ambiguous and the remainder unsure of the truth of any subject. A former President, one of our Founding Fathers, John Adams, has been quoted as saying, "I have come to the conclusion that one useless man is a sham, two is a law firm and three or more is a congress."

We are told, morality has no role in the administration of justice. Well that burns any question of requiring ethical considerations by our judiciary. The human emotion factor is one that has too long affected the direct application of the law, as currently written. When the needs of society and the call for change become evident, it is then dependent on the legislature to correct deficiencies. There have been suggestions that Islamic "sharia law" might serve the needs of certain minority, legal issues. Such a move to utilizing specific elements of Islamic based legal process, would be the most potentially destructive attack on the U.S. judicial system since its inception. To the proponents of sharia law, I adamantly declare, without caveat, as to any adaptation of other legal formats we must always remember, First Amendment liberties are not derived from international law but rather from the United States Constitution's Bill of Rights.

Unlike other forms of government, the unique position of Congress and the two party system, appears for many, the reason for discordance in Washington. The lack of, or inability to compromise and cohabit in resolving critical issues, may emphasize why our legislatures, nationally and state wide, constantly fail to represent their constituencies, as promised during campaigning. Our current legislative impasse could be phrased as follows; they talk without listening and then listen without hearing. Regrettably it has been proven that some children do not play well with others.

The inevitable question; is it time for a strong, vote achieving third or fourth party, to allow greater choice at each election? The process to create such an emerging threat to the standing power structures is complicated enough, requiring compliance to the myriad of regulations in each state. As common our current legislative insufficiency might be, it is we the voting populace who are at fault. We continually send so many morally and ethically undisciplined and patently self-engrossed individuals to Congress and our state legislatures. The cost of electioneering and the clawing by special interest groups to acquire a prominent position in the candidate's declarations, merely fuels this dysfunction in the Halls of Congress.

I believe the intent of our founders was as caretakers of a new system of government. The functions of the three branches have, as a sole obligation, to both secure and keep sacred the need of the people. And in that, to assure their freedoms are never compromised. "There is no higher law than the Constitution," spoke, William Henry Seward, in his March 11, 1850 speech in the US Senate. This I feel was an admonition our current and former President, past two Attorney Generals, the Supreme Court and the entire body of our national legislature should never forget. Of all the subjects covered over the years in legislative chambers, and before the judiciary, only three have provoked the undying animus of opponents and the insatiable curiosity of the media. They are, freedom of speech, freedom of religion and personal rights of the individual against that of the society wherein the individual resides. To deny by legislative act or executive fiat or judicial restraint, these freedoms, is to violate the basic tenets of a democratic nation.

Often, the courts will proclaim they neither do nor can they do anything in the making of law. They contend they merely interpret any law in relationship to its position within the constitutional structure. Their critics argue their constant decisions, altering existing language in the Constitution and common legal use over the decades, are clear acts of their unauthorized interdiction. For years, the judicial system has been urged by the more liberal elements to use a new sense of responsibility in interpreting the original design of the Constitution in order to meet societal evolution. This distain for their primary obligation disregards the overall benefit of the people they are sworn to protect. Instead of having the Constitution rewritten through judicial fiat, desired change should be effected through the legally proscribed method to amend.

Even more interesting when reviewing the Supreme Court's tendency to overstep its Constitutional limitations, is when one remembers that a former Sr. Associate Justice, Hugo Black, was, at one time, an active member of the Ku Klux Klan. That relationship ended only when higher public position was sought and the white robes and hoods would no longer stand public scrutiny. A brief look at senatorial seniority reveals the supposed venerable, Senator Robert Byrd of Virginia, was also a sworn member of the Klan. Another curious revelation is markedly cogent. Most of the longest serving members of the Senate, came from the Democratic controlled south and the redundantly liberal enclave of Massachusetts and New York. No real conclusion, merely another political oddity.

The Crew of the Ship of Fools

More current is the question of the individual citizen's right to privacy from the prying eyes of the media, and those money generated voyeurs, referred to as the `paparazzi'. But then, if one becomes an assumed public figure, a celebrity in the arts, entertainment, sports or political arena, it becomes inevitable that one becomes fair bait for the jackals of the long lens.

The privacy issue has become paramount in today's flurry of increasing personal identity theft and government sanctioned sophisticated electronic surveillance. Where does national security begin and personal protection from intrusion, by whatever means, end? This is the dilemma faced by both legislatures and law enforcement. The horrific incidents of September 11, 2001, have heightened public awareness to our nation's vulnerability. To those who look upon the United States as a symbol of modern imperialism and moral debauchery, each new act of violence our enemies perpetrate on innocent citizens, bring renewed demands for instant retaliation on offenders and tighter and more aggressive means to protect this country.

Still, the obverse decries any attempt to investigate and intercept personal communications as a vast conspiracy to deny human rights. Is there a balance that would provide a modicum of privacy, to assure a degree of personal comfort and the ability to reveal our dedicated enemies? Only when you elect legislators and they appoint administrators, who themselves, understand and equate both poles of this controversy with equal vigor and conscientious concern, can reason permeate this controversy.

Every two years, an event unheralded throughout the past histories of other nations, Election Day, provides the American citizen an opportunity to voice their desire to change or augment through their support of supplicant legislative candidates. Every four years, we can justify or attempt to change the mantle of presidential leadership. The principle is clear. If we do not exercise what power we have, however small that power may seem to be, we ourselves then become powerless.

The critical response by a majority of the citizenry to the new government sponsored health care and the misuse of so-called "stimulus funding," had further polarized opposing groups. Whether it is called the "Tea party", or any other citizen action force, one glaring gaffe by the left leaning media and recently past national administration has occurred, as they tout these voices as the ranting of the uninformed. The previous President's advisors, and his own political party, lacked the understanding of the populace they are supposed to represent, and to whom they owed their position. No political administration can reach the people by thrusting forth caustic rebuttals to any proposal by the opposing party. Rather, they should reach out the hand of moderation, offering compromise. However, I'm afraid that may not be part of the lesson plan used in the law classes at Harvard or Columbia. Sleeping tigers do awake from time to time and riding them may make for an exhilarating experience, but dismounting can be a most dangerous act.

Peeping Into the Halls of the Elite

One flaw can be noted in the wall of inclusion built by the tenure granted so many members of higher education's professorial ranks. It overtly permits an indoctrinating influence in whatever is that individual's particular leaning – practical or political. With this guaranteed immunity from most administrative penalties, those with this vaunted tenure can, without concern, install an influence too often in disagreement with the intent of those funding the young minds in attendance. It is the general belief of most parents that they send their children to college to be educated – not indoctrinated. The purveyors of personal bias, too often inculcate thought in their instruction, often so variant with social norm, as can create a society at odds with itself through succeeding generations. Here we grant right of opinion and expression, unassailable, because of the precept of academic freedom and the ever present mantle of tenure.

Here's another fast pitch to either take a swing at or avoid and contact. Why not congressional term limitations? The President is restricted to a total of eight years for fear by some lesser informed that longer stints might create a form of dictatorship. And I don't necessarily disagree with that stricture in residency. However, a quick review of Congressional membership reveals a number of the current inhabitants have been in place from twenty to over forty years. Some have never having actually held a full-time working position in any other activity but that particular taxpayer supported government employment. A suggestion – as you knew I would have one – specific limits for both the House and Senate. Say, for the Senate – three full terms, eighteen years – and then a hiatus of six years during which they are not allowed other government paid employment or permitted position as a lobbyist among their former fellow legislators. After that, another three term limit and so on.

As for the five hundred thirty plus members of the House, an initial run of no more than eight consecutive terms. Then a hiatus for the next four years, during which they are prohibited from further supping at the federal taxpayer trough or as a lobbyist to their former colleagues. After that, again, the same conditions. Interesting concept, wouldn't you say? But then it would inhibit all those juicy perks, relatively reduced working hours, full medical benefits and of course – what would they do without that enhanced pension plan. Too bad. Might make them what our Founding Fathers earlier felt was the actual role of the elected representative, a dedicated individual willing to spend just a few years serving his fellow citizens. Of course that could open up a few more positions at unemployment and resume preparation firms which would help cut down the long lines of those now discovering they have to find a real job.

To the Walls Protecting Us from Them

My major concern with the present jurisprudence system is the flexibility of the law in judging the severity of certain offences as compared to the minimization of particular sentences. Too great a latitude is given criminals who obtain plea bargains to save the jurisdiction responsible for the prosecution, money saving avenues by not prosecuting to the full extent. We recognize the cost and time savings achieved with an already clogged court calendar, but the costs of early release of predatory offenders is a price their future victims must pay. So many celebrities and religious figures mouth less empathy for the victim, too often providing more support for the perpetrator. I worry; does nobility of purpose truly offset culpability for one's acts? Or does pursuing supposed rightful causes justify wrong doing? And as for certain religious offenders, does being originally righteous allow one to be absolved of having committed unrighteous acts?

The continual demand for greater rights for the incarcerated, than their victims, bespeaks the supposedly "coolness" of the liberally liberated mélange. To countenance the murderous acts of Mumia Abdul, to grant semi celebrity status to the Boston Race bomber, the Charles Manson's and the list of individuals more deserving the needle, becomes too lengthy and nauseous. Their possible traumatic childhoods, their inability to succeed in normal society and the misguided naiveté of their new found fans, is far more heralded than the loss suffered by their victim's families and friends. But isn't this just another part of the perverted genetic makeup of the ultra-liberal sycophant?

Now for a moment, back to the legislative temples. Let us again speak to the cacophony of misspeak; referring to our national legislators and the many moles who work in the dark holes of a government bureaucracy. A bureaucracy that has exasperated generations and depleted the federal pocketbook for decades? Truth is always a personal interpretation by the speaker, a proclivity to interpreting every requested response to someone else's original comment – the semantic tool most befitting political speakers. I love the age old quip regarding the pontificating so prevalent in Congress. "A friend told me he'd gone to hear a certain elected official speak at his club. Spoke for over an hour," my friend reported. "What did he talk about," I asked. "Don't know," my friend answered, he didn't say."

It is amusing that elected legislators at all levels seem to make sense to their supporters before they get elected. Yet, once ensconced in their position, begin a campaign of convoluted commentary, seeking out public awareness through the media for their sudden change in philosophical direction. This confusion is their shield against a definition of who they may really be. However it remains, the politician to a TV camera is much like the dog to a fireplug – neither can ever pass one without taking personal advantage.

Attempting to understand the logjam that so symbolizes the legislative process in Washington, it is important for the citizenry to recognize, we are dealing with 535 individuals we've naively and at times, unknowingly elected to a totally dysfunctional organization. Thus, with their seeming inability to compromise, all we can expect is legislative constipation and rhetorical diarrhea.

Now, a Truly Disingenuous Failure

The United Nations was created to provide a global forum for sharing viewpoints, representation of the universal population and as a platform to review, discuss and resolve worldwide conflicts. When the need does arise to take action or share responsibility, their continuing requirement of individual national sovereignty becomes a drama of loosely related members of an evidently dysfunctional family. No body of representative interests has ever engendered such continuing dialogue, proposed so much, promised so little and accomplished nothing. They exhibit a continuing mixed menu of malcontents. They build sand castles of declarations, knowing full well that the next tide of posturing and demand for personal advantage through the veto vote, will immediately destroy what had too often been proclaimed earlier as a tribute to compromise.

The face of mutual respect is a mask worn by all who desire dominance, rather than determination. The United Nations is not a center for compromise, rather an international debating society and poorly imagined at that. It is merely a congregation of ideologues and the representatives of potential enemies of the United States. Viewing the General Assembly seating area, one can see the hundred and ninety plus nations, each with identification embossed on their nameplates. The identical sizing of each of these nameplates is the only sense of equality many of the smaller nations have. A number of so-called nations are minuscule enough to be dwarfed in size by many of the states in our country. Many others are dependent on the charity or politically demanded support and largesse by larger, more dominant members. Smaller members are orphans of rebellion, coups and the ever evolving familia' of nepotism, founded through violence and intimidation of their constituency.

Should the United Nations be handed their collected luggage of venal intrigue and hollow declarations, and told to take the proverbial `hike'? To find another country in which to propagate their arrogantly espousing image and continue to wail against the winds of their own making? Throwing this addled assembly of egomaniacs into the troubled waters of another country, might easily create even greater global misdeeds. At least it would save the New York City police from the egregious attitude and actions of the UN's diplomatic coterie of clowns who have never seen an illegal parking space they wouldn't violate.

In the history of man, no more lasting impact is ever experienced than a war. Throughout mankind's time on this planet, more lives have been lost in religious wars, even considering the horrific carnage of WW II. Thirty million slain, of which millions were Jews. Included in the mass homicide would be Gypsies, political dissidents, homosexuals, the physically and mentally disadvantaged, and others whose personal beliefs and lifestyles conflicted with the tyrannical dictate of the former Corporal and failed artist, Adolph Hitler. Still not to forget the millions opposing the murderous, freedom denying ideology of the Communist reign. Still perishing in the infamous Gulags created by Josef Stalin, becoming a part of forgotten masses lost in the bleakness of Siberia.

However, aside from the statistics of these conflicts, we are told it is not the primary intent of waging war to just kill the enemy, but additionally to seek added land, wealth and/or human commodity in slaves. But first, and foremost, to inflict terror on the opposition. With that installed as an overpowering imagery, embedded in the psyche of the opponent, it becomes a tool for conquest and domination. Historically, it was the goal of one combatant to decimate the other combatant by constant assault or to deny the substance of existence, or the means to wage a defense through siege or embargo supported by other nations.

Fear is a resource to help override the initial desire to resist. Rarely is compromise part of the language of the participants and that leads directly to the multiplying tragedies of all conflicts. Had they first been willing to talk, to listen, possibly reaching some degree of compromise . . . but then, such foolish hyperbole? Regrettably, written history has assured us, it is the nature of man to demand through force what has been driven by greed.

There exists the pretense that the law is a system of known rules, applied by a judiciary. This is not true, since legal rules are never clear, yet we expect clear meaning prior to judgment. We are faced with a constant social vacillation assuring us that justice should be tempered by mercy when required. Mercy is a human emotion, while judicial rulings are the submission of fact to legal review. Samaritans do not belong in the courtroom and dedicated givers of sympathy should never populate a jury unless their concern might more favor the proven victims of the accused. Justice, Sir Hugh L. Markby of the British controlled Indian High Court, wrote in his 1889 work, "The Elements of Law," stated succinctly, "The value of law lies not in the happiness it creates, but rather the misery and suffering it prevents."

The Media, Milestone to Truth, or Labyrinth of Deceit

We cannot have freedom without a free press. But with that onerous prerogative and normally unfettered power, must be a sense of fairness in reporting incidents and situations. Devotion to an impartial recitation of the facts, as had been or are being revealed, must be the mantra for all those who declare themselves journalists. We cannot tell the journalist what to write or the broadcast media what to report. Unfortunately that earlier tradition of mandated fairness has become the ashes of a fire, originally set to light the unknown and seek the truth. During the past several decades, the profession of journalism has been devaluated for ratings and circulation.

Editors have become publishing pimps, allowing the whorish nature of unrestrained reporters and feature writers to damage the traditional image of equal treatment in all submissions. Once a much heralded profession, which had used its freedom of speech to pursue the wrongs felt by the populace, it had the power to uncover corruption and maintain light on the doings of our elected and appointed officials, marking our unique democratic status throughout the world. Discouraging as it is, they too have cast their lot with liberal ideologues as well as their slobbering subservience to certain pas national administration.

The worker bees in the increasing number of cable news networks, would have us believe they are `vox populi', the voice of the people. First, we are required to accept their constant protestations of fairness and truth above any improper influence. In the competitive cat fight known as news broadcasting, this fairness declaration is an expression, tinged with sarcasm, and at times, ironic equilibrium. A few have been identified earlier in this writing, but to name just a few of these, might appear a possible disservice to the growing plethora of presumed pundits. We live in an age prolific with pseudo advisors on every subject imaginable, be it politics, science, religion and the ever embarrassing subtlety of personal relationships, including the previously limited aspects of bodily hygiene and sexual proclivities.

Three of the major broadcast networks, in their constant fawning over a previous President, must now face the truth of their espoused journalistic ethics. Did they factually report what happened during his administration – both the effective and the insufficient, equally? It is difficult for journalists to cower and bow obsequiously for more than eight years, while attempting to take notes for the next story. Bias is a wart on the face of the speaker when he or she declares a claim of fairness being the only excuse for an expressed opinion. I remember the old joke line, "How can you tell when a politician is lying; when you see his lips moving?" And when you can tell a journalist is residing into the calm of bias during an interview? When he or she stops writing and begins to nod in agreement to what is being said.

Shamefully, the leftist leaning part of our society often borders the extreme edge of buffoonery, reflected in the continuing media popularity among a few of those still not institutionalized. When the media crosses that very thin, and at times, wavy line as to fact or fabrication, and the government is the target, national security issues arise as a barricade against further inspection by that media. Yet, when the verbal or written onslaught is aimed toward a private individual, no such protection seems to exist. When criticized for a specific character assassination, the offending media becomes the champion of the First Amendment freedom of speech doctrine. However, that safeguard fails to appear for the targeted individual, leaving that individual figuratively naked in the light of public scrutiny. It creates an immediate situation where, if found to be completely of no guilt, he or she is never able to fully regain their personal honor or reputation.

Free speech means anyone can write or say ignorant, stupid or hateful statements under the umbrella of Constitutional protection, and that my friends is the price of the liberty we so cherish. However, there is a rarely discussed portion of the Constitution that has been, for years, a source of devalued ethics in the hallowed Halls of Congress. "Article I, Section 6, first paragraph," has too long been the vehicle for abuse of the First Amendment guarantee of free speech. The final lines of that segment states, ". . . and for any speech or debate in either House, they shall not be questioned in any other place." This gives any swaggering, self-aggrandizing member of Congress, the right, while on the floor of the House or Senate, to declare, state, proclaim, defame and utter unverified accusations, that outside those two locations could be defined as slander. Moreover, when placed in the sacrosanct Congressional Record, becomes even more a part of a misconstrued history.

A recent example, a senior Senator, during the 2012 Presidential campaign, quoted a claim provided him by someone he refused to identify, casting an accusation on the opposition party's candidate. A statement that was totally false and without validation, and for which he veritably could not be admonished or punished. Did he apologize? Of course not, immediately veiling himself in that same bit of wordage in the Constitution? In this writer's opinion, the overt action of a coward. It is unfortunate that he represented the beautiful state of Nevada at the time of his egregious lies.

For those desiring recourse in the courts relative to such emanations, the escutcheon of free speech, as promised in the Constitution, and that particular passage, will be raised on high by the offending legislator. And were any specifically false or unjustified utterances to ever reach a court hearing - a near impossibility - the brothers – and sisters - in black robes, would most likely rule the target of such legislative abuse to be a "public figure." Two hundred years ago would have resolved such situations. Pistols at twenty feet – no further conversation.

To counterbalance the pedantic nature of either viewpoint in any discussion by the media, there exists the inviolable axiom of my personal making; "If the government is not subject to continual review, most certainly subjugation of the people by that government, can and will occur."

The renowned Supreme Court Associate Justice, Hugo Black, wrote, "Only a free and unrestrained press can effectively expose deception in government." Many journalists adopt a mantle of righteousness which they constantly append to their declared position of neutrality. However, words do have consequences, and those who write or converse publicly through the print and electronic media, must accept that neutrality can only be accomplished within a guaranteed true report of fact.

With the entry of the "blog" into the communications arena, coupled as mentioned earlier, those electronic trip wires of trite and uncorroborated prattle, force us to face a blizzard of commentary, heedless as to fact or personal subjectivity. The Internet has given voice to a flurry of statements, rebuttals and contradiction, which at best creates confusion out of what once was a diverse dialogue. The ever expanding "blogosphere" and its social compatriots have provided new, and as yet, uncontrolled assaults on the freedoms of speech and protection from libel and slander. Such Blogs and tweets', snapchats' and "Facebook" pronouncements, are too often the belching of the uninformed and gastric utterances of the ignorant.

A journalist, by close interpretation of the original word, meant chronicler, reporter and observer. Today, liberal media proponents claim a right to dissect and provide the "real meaning" of what has occurred. Unfortunately, but so evident with any news regarding violent or suspicious death or disaster oriented incidents, the initial disclosure is controlled by the long held dictate; "If it bleeds, it leads," whether on the front page or the prime time TV and radio news.

The tabloids make excellent momentary reading while waiting for minimally paid, and often disinterested checkout clerks at the grocery store, to complete their monotonous duties. We have seen such print purveyors of rumor, scandal mongering and salacious misstatement, excoriated by others for their supposed lack of professional and moral concern. But then again, we relish the tidbits about entertainment figures whose normal position in society, without such pop culture exposure, would be far more mundane than can be imagined. The trackers and writers of such juvenile journals, are good in what they do. Unlike the garbage collectors who gather human waste in bulk form, the tabloids retain each odorous item for later revelation. Instead of relegating all these bits of the inconsequential for the landfill, they are presented as fact or possibly containing a potential semblance of truth. However, more like the carnivores of the vast African plain, seeking the unwary prey, they wait in stealth to pick out their target of choice, looking for the slightest inattention in that target.

Any weakness in a character or opportune moment, provides these human waste collectors the opportunity to pounce on the subject of the moment. Yet, without the desire by a public for the smallest details of transgression, error, inopportune physical position or bizarre behavior, such tabloids, would be relegated to the bottom of bird cages. Before we castigate these pawnbrokers of petty human frailty, we must remember. To the wannabe celebrity or the established personality, such printed swill is the fodder that engorges the hungry fan – the constituency that must be constantly fed the staple of their personal fantasies. It is this narcissistic nature and drive for acclaim, regardless of the lack of talent or suspect personal behavior, that drives this zeal in the celebrity for recognition – a self-imposed façade against the reality of being human – just like the rest of us.

The Halls of Congress Where Lay Shadows of Deception

Legislators should be held to the highest level of veracity and professional ethics. Humorist Mark Twain wrote, "Suppose you were an idiot. And suppose you were a member of Congress. But then, I have repeated myself." Thomas Jefferson once wrote, "When an individual first considers running for public office, the rottenness begins." As I have verbalized earlier, I am a firm believer in a constituted term limit structure for all elected officials of the state and national level. Thus, here goes, beating my head against the formidable, and to date, the unassailable wall of Congressional resistance to change. As concerns seeking public office, too often many potential candidates are adverse to run for office. There is the cost, the time required from personal business enterprise and the inevitable investigative intrusion into one's personal life. Miniscule matters from long past, that if revealed, still becomes grist for the mill of political opportunism. It has long been contended, the quickest and least expensive way to track your ancestry is to run for public office. The media will perform that task, politically oriented hatchet in hand.

Today we have members of the national legislature who have literally never worked in any other profession than as an elected official. Where I ask is their understanding of the many problems that constitute the daily worries, concerns and stress faced by their constituency? And to add legitimacy to the entire electoral process, once an individual, a Governor, a Senator or Representative, announces his or her candidacy for the presidency, he or she should, no less than six months prior to Election Day, resign from the office they currently hold. That resignation would be based on their publicly agreed intent to continue in the race as a viable candidate.

Again, prime examples of this phlegmatic tenure concept were Senators Robert Byrd of Virginia, who spent 51 years in both House and Senate; Strom Thurmond, from South Carolina, 47 years; Daniel Inouye, Hawaii, 16 days short of 50 years, which included House and Senate. An additional list of both Democratic and Republican tenure includes another 17 members of the Senate serving from thirty-six to over forty years each. Ted Kennedy, spent well over 46 years in the Senate, and based on his age, biography and wealth, he apparently never had any other occupation.

But let us not forget our friends in the House. Among the other algae of longstanding occupancy are, Charles Rangel, (D), New York and, Nancy Pelosi (D), California, former Speaker of the House. Of the present 435 residents of the congressional halls, over fifty have been nesting there for 10 or more terms. And to those young students still applying to Harvard, Columbia, Princeton or other landfills of liberal waste, that category equals 20 to 40 years each. No wonder the reported unemployment figure is getting so low – everyone is either in Congress or working for them.

Critics to my suggestions will argue that the longer one remains in the legislature, the greater wisdom and understanding are achieved. What the opponents to my reasoning fail to recognize is the inevitable seepage of potential corruption and enrichment of their personal fortunes at taxpayer expense over such a prolonged residency in the protective arms of our national legislature. "They sacrifice to serve us," some will say. "They could have earned much more in private enterprise," is another contention. "They have gained power in status to effect more substantive legislation." Now that's another of the uninformed comments by the sheep that follow the media Judas goats. The voter, not aware as to the insufficiencies of many members of national and state legislatures, still continually retain them in office.

The Congressional salaries are not exceedingly large, but the added health, life insurance, pension and ancillary expense allowances are far more that John Q. Public is warranted or guaranteed. Notwithstanding these public reimbursements, why do so many members leave office with such measurably increased financial assets? Just asking – nothing implied or inferred.

Public service has lost its original intent and meaning. But rather than face the unrelenting scrutiny of a media, that can quickly turn inspection into inquisition, many potentially, well deserving candidates, will shun the intense public light focused on them. Like starving sharks in a maelstrom of feeding frenzy, the media too often allows incompetence and duality of morals to become the criteria for candidacy to elected office. Such increased legislative status merely covers an individual's plan to retain that power and influence, normally not feasible in private life, and the overriding desire to remain becomes paramount.

Even more exemplary of this continuation of incompetence and mediocrity are the throngs of state legislators, who are at best, too often ill-fitted to be representative of anything more than their own self inflation. Many state legislatures only sit in session for periods of forty to fifty days, every two years; too little time to consider, digest and develop intelligent reasoning on the hundreds of bills brought before them for debate.

During past presidential campaigns, it was revealed that candidates had amassed hundreds of millions of dollars in campaign donations. And for this we received hours of placation of supporters, impossible promises for the non-committed and more metaphors and prosaic blathering than a television evangelist. Sums, I feel, could possibly assure several childhood diseases being vanquished. Monies that could provide educational benefits to hundreds of thousands of children, today deprived of even the most basic enhancements to provide them a reasonable window of opportunity. An equally upsetting fact is that many candidates on state and local level will have garnered literally hundreds of thousands in campaign funds. Lose or withdraw earlier, they retain these citizen provided funds yet unspent. Why not have that money placed in escrow in their political party's coffers for use to support the next candidate? Too simple, or too quick to remove the lure of post-election personal gain? I had a feeling that was too rational a suggestion.

Walking Among False Gods

As mentioned earlier, I spent a majority of my life in the sports, entertainment and convention facility management industry. That, and my link to a number of major international sports events and professional sports operations, provided me an opportunity to view a part of the playgrounds of modern public deities.

What I've found was both illuminating, and at times, discouraging. We in the industry were constantly exposed to a vast array of entertainment and athletic notables. I quickly admit here, I have never, nor could ever accomplish what many of them do or have achieved, the musician, artist, the actor, the dancer, the singer, the athletic star. But my experience quickly taught me one irrefutable fact. Without the coterie of directors, stagehands, event technicians, the arrangers, the trainers, the coaches, management personnel, the publicists and the many other unseen, less reimbursed and too often disregarded support staff, the desired result by the individual or group of performers or athletes would be impossible.

Sana these many helpers, the performers would find themselves alone in empty rehearsal halls or twanging on borrowed guitars in family garages. Potential sports icons would be forced to display their talents on practice fields and courts and ice rinks, devoid of spectators and cheering fans. Fortunately there are many truly talented artists in the demanding entertainment disciplines and those superb athletes who added a sense of nobility in achieving their accomplishments. Sadly, they are too often overshadowed by the misdeeds and exhibitionism of less than average achievers in the arts and on the sports platform. I've had the opportunity to meet with a number of personalities whose abilities and public personas reflected their quality as both performer and human being. Those meetings and conversations have added so much to my enjoyment of their accomplishments and deserved accolades, coupled with a dedication to my profession.

It is said the cream will always rise to the top, but in the instance of that milieu of untalented pseudo celebrities, I believe it has been curdled by the inane public acceptance of the bizarre. Second rate and exaggerated performance styles are pronounced by entertainment industry journals as exceptional. The areas of professional basketball and football have become havens for too many misguided, egocentric and verifiable sociopaths, who continue their activities under the guise of a bargaining agreement, forced on weak team ownership by overly aggressive agents and a self-serving player's union.

There are too many athletes who spawn one illegitimate child after another, abuse their wives or girlfriends – or both. Indulge or deal in drugs, become addicted to alcohol and other travesties of moral imbalance. A year, perhaps two in college, paid for by donor funding and after a statistically successful season, it's off to the pros. There a particular number will become very wealthy. Here's a suggestion from one of the public herd. How about returning a sum twice the athletic scholarship cost back to the school that gave them their opportunity to access the pros? Thus assisting other young people deserving of an academic opportunity and who may not be interested in advancing immediately to the ranks of the raunchy rich.

This small group of semi juvenile miscreants, represent what is flawed in that industry. If any of we less exalted individuals, committed just one of those offenses referred to earlier, we would soon be on the street, unemployed or headed to rehabilitation or possibly, incarceration. Yet, time after time these arrogant, excessively paid individuals, are given a second chance, and a third, and a fourth, infinitum. And the eventual payee is the fan whose ticket costs have risen astronomically over the past four decades.

May I once more offer another thought from the hinterlands, which just might limit or at least diminish such off the field or court behavior? A heavy hit on their income the first time unless becoming eligible for incarceration or suspension from participation – and in those two latter instances, no payment in any form. Then, a year off the field or court or ice. Fire them after they have screwed up the second time. Assure they cannot be employed by another team immediately and put them on a reasonably manageable probationary period, after which they can again apply to join the ranks of the athletic anointed – and I emphasize *apply*. Make them accept and abide by the same legal and moral restrictions we all must deal with in our daily lives. Reinstate the employer/employee relationship that is the standard in the real world. In the professional athletics' ranks, it has become apparent the inmates are in charge of the institution.

I Love What Others Say; Even Myself

As stated before, the written word has a structure that can withstand the vagaries of cultural progression and time. Its original shape and form changes only within man's interpretation as time and thought evolves and that is affected by the times in which the reader dwells. There must exist accountability to the reading and viewing public that demands adherence to basic codes of honesty in providing details and preparation of the material. Without such a requirement, the media will continue to merely be the indiscriminate mouthing of malcontents. They continue insisting the public is too inferior in intellect to understand the written word unless first filtered by those contending a superior position in society.

Recognizing I've commented on a number of subjects, I would ask your permission to allow a focus on an activity with which I've had a lengthy personal and up close experience.

One evening I watched a two-hour segment of the History Channel, one of my favorite television offerings. It dealt with the so-called "Hippie Era", a time during which I was in my mid-thirties to early fifties career tenure, basically on the fringe through hosting many major concert events as a facility executive. More recently, a growing number of former rock artists and their fellow band mates have reappeared on the pop music scene. It's rather quixotic to see these aging, former icons, hair fast diminishing, greying or totally absent. Their paunches sagging like an overloaded cow before milking, striving to relive the peak of their popularity. Strangely enough, they still have often succeeded in bringing out the multitudes they once enjoyed. However, their audiences mirror their own aging if not dissipated visages.

During that earlier period, as the director of large public assembly facilities, I found myself in the midst of the anti-Vietnam War, pro whale's advocacy, antiestablishment chaos and the pseudo guru Timothy Leary's drug laced 'awakening period'. I have heard and read so much of the anguish their followers suffered regarding the deaths of such rock music luminaries as, Jimi Hendrix, Janis Joplin, the "Doors" lead, Jim Morrison and Curt Cobain. True, they were the epitome of that particular music genre, but they also represented a form of entertainment too often devoted to pure narcissistic exhibitionism. Their art form was often dependent on bizarre behavior, accompanied by excessive sound and lyrics few could hear, much less understand. Regardless, their popularity and star status among their particular fan demographics, represented a rising generation of hedonism. Self-indulgence is a common human failing, but the rock music era tried its best to breach the envelope time and time again.

In the early part of the 1960's, the English wonder kids from Liverpool, the Beatles, burst on the music scene. I had the pleasure and privilege of being a host facility manager for two of their concerts toward the end of their final tour. Gentlemen, they were, appearing as respectful and true performers, demanding little and expecting to perform to their best for their adoring fans. One of the reasons for their successful appearances was their manager, Brian Epstein, a gentleman of a high English order, a true professional. With his death, I sincerely believe the beginning of the end for the Beatle phenomena and started its speedy decline. It was his management skill, the protective coating and ever present antibody that kept the foursome in the limelight in a manner acceptable to fans of all ages.

With Epstein gone, the susceptibility to foreign intrusion by damaging influences began. First, there was the foursomes near public worship at the feet of the Indian Guru Maharishi Yogi, a Hindu trickster, who unlike legitimate, religious figures in India, charged the gullible celebrities for a cacophony of indistinct babble. And, of course, then there was the introduction to John Lennon of Yoko Ono, who apparently sought a free train ride to fame and acceptance she might never have known. With her entry into the Beatle fold, the disintegration of the group's former cohesiveness led to the quartet's breakup, not long after. With Lennon's tragic and untimely assassination by a demented fan, his widow proceeded to continually reinvent her famous husband, wanting to assure her place, ill deserved, among the celebrity fold. A rather crude joke during that time reflected many opinions about her use of Lennon's well-earned legacy. A comment I am merely passing on to the reader; "What is similar between a starving African refugee and Yoko Ono? They've both have learned to survive off a dead beetle."

During the violence prone period of the late sixties to the mid-eighties, the younger generation had many self-anointed Gurus. Each month the media proclaimed a new "messiah for the misguided masses." Anything that frustrated the post war domesticity and passive public demeanor was grist for the mill of ticket sales. But then again, that was the business and we in the entertainment facility industry knew it and accepted its conditions as part of the constant struggle to maximize programming. That meant acquiring what was hot on the music charts, what the primary patron wanted and would accept as their next pseudo Mammon to adore.

During this time, as expected, legal challenges would occur regarding the facility industry's attempt to minimize the introduction of alcohol, drugs and weapons into their concert venues. The ACLU, *the American Civil Liberties Union*, became the banner carrier for those who felt such searches and inquiries at facility turnstiles were an unacceptable intrusion and in violation of individual

Constitutional rights. Complaints were heard, legal actions instituted and case law recorded. The ability of facility managers to protect their structures and that of the public welfare, health, safety and security, was often diminished in favor of strangely interpreted freedom of expression rulings by local and district courts. Compromise was offered but refused by supporters of unlimited right of access. The aftermath was a watering down of existing entry regulations, an obeisance to a badly misinterpreted Constitutional question by the judiciary, continuing until that fateful date – `9/11'.

I consider myself fortunate to have basically phased out of the direct facility management industry when the newest music mania became de rigueur. "Rap" and its companion, the even more insidious, "Gangsta Rap," became the image presented to a youthful African American generation. Personally, I consider "rap" to be the attempt by the untalented to achieve notoriety while exhibiting a remarkable level of insufficiency in the performing arts. The only good thing is, you can't whistle it. So there, you've heard another aging dinosaur bellowing and totally unaware of the younger generation's new vision – or flaw – whichever.

Today, outlandish and freakish is the chic format for many Hollywood celebrities. Erratic, wild or unpredictable has become the nom de plume for younger entertainers desiring the glare of public notice with the aid of the ever present flash of paparazzi cameras. But something needs to be said here. There was another element of society that inadvertently aided to this confluence of ambition, greed and personal aggrandizement. The "they" I refer to is the "other generation," the group that fought to keep this country free during WW II and ensuing conflicts. They were the electorate who allowed legislators to weaken restraints to such actions at that time. A lessening of personal public discipline that has exacerbated with today's millennials. A judiciary, who displayed the backbone of a jellyfish in constantly submitting to the ACLU and other ultra-liberal advocate demands for a society free of any degree of self-discipline or rational human protocol. A continuing demand for unlimited access to excessively expanded, often misinterpreted freedoms, without restraint or any degree of self-control.

However, attitudes change when the tiger is at the gate, as has been reflected in recent years due to the increasing incidents of violence from both foreign and domestic sources. I respect and feel the First Amendment of the US Constitution is the cornerstone of our system of government. However, when public interest is overwhelmed by individual demands for personal preference, regardless of the deleterious effect on the public as a group, there must be a reasonable degree of judicial restraint. Otherwise, we once again free the hungry fox into the chicken house.

I Have Now Moved From My Spot on the Curb

Am I opinionated? You bet your 'bippy', as one of the participants used to say on a very popular comedy show, years past. Otherwise, I wouldn't have had the genital appendages to make all the comments I have penned within. I open myself to all the outrage and angry responses the Constitution allows others to hurl. Yet, to save the reader time, it would be best to consolidate my thoughts. It would possibly make it a lot easier for my critics to rail forth – at least with a particle of sequential envy. They can borrow a copy of, or hopefully, buy a copy of this book and merely move to this portion. Now on to a summary of what my addled thinking (which, no doubt, many will consider all these following comments) has conjured up as the basis of my personal soliloquy.

The perversion of the original Islamic ideology by the current fanatic misfits who claim their right to a Jihadist movement, is the most dangerous and potentially destructive threat faced by the United States in recent decades and endangers all democratic societies. It is plainly reminiscent of the brutality of Adolph Hitler and his Nazi regime. It is the Black Plague of ideologies. The stench of misguided, religious fanaticism. Even if not the will and support of the majority of peaceful intending Muslims, such fanaticism and resulting savagery against the innocent will bring continuing suffering, domination and death, if allowed to expand its reach. Until the mainstream Islamic follower and their more influential clerics, condemn and eradicate this ongoing ravage by the more dissident elements, they will always be the target for distrust, rejection and hoped for destruction by others. Like the viper, the poisonous snake, it must be destroyed by first removing its radical ideological head.

As for the evangelical, supposed charismatic Christian movement, it must reduce its strident calls for damnation of anyone and anything that opposes their particular views. If not, religion in America will continue to share with race, as the two most divisive forces in society. As can be quickly assumed, I don't like halleluiah shouting cash cows that bellow and rant, doing little more than bolstering their own egos. To me, that defiles the very sanctity of people's individual desire for a closer communion with whatever God they wish. It immolates their very spirit and mental consciousness with rhetoric and gaudy show, more adapted to the carnival circuit.

Let me now clarify to the best of my ability my personal position as refers to religion as is an integral part of American society. I am a strong advocate of the right of others to profess their religious beliefs, so long as they do not trespass over two defined lines of demarcation. Assert and proclaim your particular beliefs, but don't attempt to forcibly impress your beliefs on others who are not your fellow adherents. And very importantly, never use your group's dominance in population or political or economic prominence in any specific area, to dictate public policy or legislative control. I can never accept any theology that defines non-believers as having less stature within the human society, or which demands such adherence of their followers as to nullify free human expression.

Of course the question of creationism versus scientific investigation of the "big bang" theory, has become a major point of contention among those declaring a Genesis like beginning and those who look for evolution as the factual history of man and the planet. I don't know from whence the earth arrived on the scene. Or man suddenly appeared or evolved. I wasn't personally there. Nevertheless, with all the contentious debate, I'm now wondering if the big bang might not have merely been God coughing.

Immigration is a nearly insurmountable flash point, as viewed by many in our country. Most Americans can claim in their background, ancestors who chose to leave their homeland, and often family, to journey to a place where they had been told one could find or make the better life. So today, we're faced with the illegal incursion of hundreds of thousands of basically Hispanic people and other minorities. A number coming from a corrupt and impoverished Mexico or other beleaguered and despotic tyrannies further south. Our southern neighbors are so beset by their own insufficiency that their governmental instability and criminal control has created a pressure, forcing so many of its citizens to leave.

This isn't new to the political scene. Earlier it was the "mick" Irish and then the "dago" Italians, the "bohunk" Hungarians, the "kike", the `kraut', and on and on. And from our not too distant past, the now forbidden "N" word. Brutal and distasteful were these references to good people, only seeking a better life, a chance for a reasonable future. But their difference, from many illegal entries today, is in some opinions, that they strove to meet the requirements and conditions of citizenship. They knew that without viable recognition, their search could be short-lived. President Theodore Roosevelt had his opinion on the entry of the many newcomers during his era when he said, "America has to be more than a polyglot boarding house. We must end the concept of a hyphenated American populace."

Today, a number of American cities have declared their environs to be "sanctuaries" to the "oppressed" but still illegal alien. These local governments ostensibly feel they are reflecting the heartfelt desire of their constituency to provide help to those needing succor and protection from a national authority. The elected officials of such "sanctuaries" have spent years demanding greater and greater share of the public fiscal largesse necessary to harbor and support these undocumented entries, all of whom are, of course, potential voters. I fear another example of the flock being led, not by a sheep of their own genus, but rather by political "Judas goats." These sanctuaries have more recently become the havens for those intent on obtaining their personal good and wealth at the cost of other human life and property. However, there is no legal standing for any community or lower jurisdiction to defy federal law. It is the sanctimonious bellowing by political forces demanding voter support by any means, regardless of its illegality.

I welcome anyone willing to accept the rules of this country, following due process in seeking citizenship. If that is not their goal, then what is the process desired by so many "hand-labor" enterprises who seek this low cost, docile worker resource? And what should be the response of the local, state and national governments regarding provision of health care, social services and the inevitable question? The question is, should Constitutional rights be provided to illegal immigrants as compared to those already citizens or those here with valid visas and the required "green card? That is a decision our legislators have never been able to make, so embroiled are they in their own petty bickering and political posturing. Even more crucial to whatever decisions might come out of all this dialogue, how will all these children entering our country be fed, or clothed or educated and to what level for their successful survival? Even the altruistic academia should recognize the simple math – what is it costing and who will be required to pay that cost?

The constant flow of varying ethnic cultures into our society reminds one of adding more different items into the proverbial stew pot, whether it be product or condiment. Thus change will happen in taste and consistency. Our country has long been referred to as a melting pot; a welcomed, diverse polymorphous of cultures, social, ethnic and economic. But has that melding nature apparently ceased, hardening the attitude of those here, against those who have come illegally or wait at border fences to enter covertly? Today we face an overt war with the Mexican drug cartels who use their best efforts to continue feeding the growing drug habit in our country. The criminal element south of the border have butchered thousands in their own country and thus have had no qualms in doing battle with our limited border defenses.

Several years earlier I provided operational planning for an organization providing specialized medical services to various groups, numerous among them schools with high rates or multicultural students. At one school I was taken aback by the large sign, proudly displayed and pointed to by the school's principal. It read, "Fifty-seven languages are spoken in our school." As diverse as they might proudly declare, how can we be expected to meet the educational needs of such a cultural and linguistic multiform without a government that recognizes and is geared to attack this growing problem with rational systems and the funding to accomplish its goals?

Addressing our current political system, we have too long endured the constant vindictive dialogue, obstructionism and at times petulance of the current dual party system. It has performed in shameless disregard of their constituencies, demanding fealty to proclaimed ideologies that are merely facades for their personal enhancement. Now, is it time to consider a possible third party structure or multiple political establishments? Would this allow a preponderance of votes and allow the winning group to select the nation's chief executive?

As referred to earlier, such an undertaking requires the financing and rearranging the ballot system in many states, a herculean task. It furthermore requires change in the tabulation of any election's final results. Possibly a three party system; a tripartite form of national representation would need to be constitutionally devised. It has been attempted to a modest degree a number of times during the history of our country. Yet the result was merely to provide one party the wherewithal to achieve the White House by the splitting of popular vote. And in the end, there would be little hope to gain the Electoral College edge required. We still need channels for the voices of the dissenter, the protestor, the iconoclast. We must assure there are voices that can be funneled into consistent political philosophies. Ideas that can be rationally reviewed by all concerned. Unless radically changing their present image and cavalier attitude toward the general good, both political parties have diminished this country's image measurably throughout the free world and the nation they have sworn to serve.

The recent Veterans Administration lack of fulfilling their obligation to those whose service have assured this country's freedom remains a stain on current and numerous past national administrations. However, those news outlets brave or ethical enough to reveal the truth, have discovered, as of this writing, reportedly only a rare several persons at the VA had been fired. And the few who have been singled out for their incompetence, lack of attention or actual misdeeds, are placed on leave pending resolution of their cases. "Placed on leave." That is the newest axiom for a paid vacation, usually lasting upwards of a year or more. By then, the union protected, civil service immunity clothed individuals, will have time to either find a different positon or decide to retire at partial or full benefits.

Our principal source for news ostensibly emanates from the New York City, "Mecca of Media." We continually hear references to the Midwestern soul of our great nation. And to the far west lies the cocoon of kooky and aberrant behavior, modeling itself as the hip and upbeat generational conclave. So let me get this straight, if New York is the intellectual head of our nation, and the Midwest is its heart, then it stands to reason, San Francisco must serve as the country's rectum.

To law enforcement, we owe an ongoing debt. As we do to those who manage the fire hoses or deliver the emergency care wherever and whenever needed. But to the controlling local and state government agencies, we should insist on a continuing and diligent watch over the procedures and tactics used by those with the badge. We ask them to constantly place themselves between us and the malefactor. They face daily dangers from the drunk, the fleeing criminal, the psychopath and the habitual domestic disturbance challenge. We owe them more than the media frenzy created at every instance of law enforcement incidents, whether accidental or actual misdeeds. Yet, they still must adhere to the highest level of appropriateness and valid restraint so as to both protect and serve all the public. Unless, and until we pay a living wage, required extensive training and on the job review and psychological oversight, we will see continuing transgressions by those mandated to protect and serve. And an increase of public disfavor and animosity toward law enforcement in all forms.

The media has become too self-endowed with a mistaken belief in their role as arbiter of public morals and judge of what is or should be the correct interpretation of what information, is in fact, news. It becomes impossible to always determine the truth, causing us to be distrustful of what we hear and see via the printed word, the radio air waves and on the television screen. We've redesigned heroes in our modern lexicon. Those in the past we heralded, are today forgotten. In their place, cartoon characters created by the entertainment world, exalted by a feckless media and magnified by a jaded juvenile populace. But to the inveterate believer in the irrefutable truthful purity of our current media, it is useless for me to prattle on. We merely ask print and electronic journalism to recognize their obligation to the truth, before their ethical transgressions become the new face of the reporting profession.

Time to Close This Out?

I've had the opportunity to live in many places throughout this great country. Regardless of the level of diversity and those social quirks unique to each and every community, we are blessed to have them as a part of the greatest nation ever devised in the history of mankind. Its dimension and scope of achievement is not marked by towering monuments to man's ego, as shadowed the social infirmities of Egypt with their pyramids and gigantic statues. Ours may not be the breadth of land once controlled by the Tsars and those vast areas under the dictatorial thumb of Chinese leadership. It is a part of this ever changing world, founded by a society, dedicated and constantly striving to assure the belief in the individual propensity for goodness, the rights of the individual being paramount and an attempt to meet the needs of its constituency, however difficult and often disputed that might be. If only time and the patience of its citizens will allow resolution of the troublesome and overcoming of the formidable.

My lifetime has seen the calm, almost docile period after WW II. Then the onset of the terrible Korean conflict. Tragically, that period was soon ripped apart by the assassination of JFK, the ensuing murder of his younger brother Robert and the principal leader of the civil rights movement, the Rev. Martin Luther King. Civil rights became the buzz word of the decade as we hurtled headlong into the jungles of Vietnam. Conflicting political reassessment and the unreasoning inability to seek compromise ran rampant for those elements at odds. I miss those days past, when the definition of right and wrong seemed so clear. It never seemed to need political incantation by legislators, interpretation by the media or curious legal justification by the courts.

Today, I find continuing fault with our current elementary to collegiate institutional schooling. Continually disparaged by teachers' union officials who wield their iron clad contracts to usurp the rights of the parent and individual instructor. It strips the earnest, professionally directed teacher little recourse; a demanding political cartel like union on one side and totally insensitive administrators and local government on the other. Until these self-protecting groups actively take a part in placing the need of the student first, they become just another barrier to reestablishing, what once was the finest freedom of educational opportunity in the world. Until their power and undue influence is modified to an acceptable degree, we will continue to allow this major disservice to the ultimate goal of what any educational system should be – the student and only the student.

Regrettably, there are too many universities and colleges that hire or sustain rabble rousing, racist spouting, literally anti American instructors and professors. They debase the purpose of education with the implementation of tenure. Use of tenure should only be granted for quality of instruction and dedication to the need of the student. We have contaminated our colleges and universities with these sycophantic adherents to personal and often convoluted opinion, devoid of reason or validity. They are protected behind an outdated and archaic system of "tenure," ironically, a word I find rhyming so closely to with manure.

I was always enamored with history, a recitation that provides us a road map along the trail from man's earliest beginnings. Today, as a subject and sometimes insufficiently required in most curriculums, it has been shunted to the back of the school bookshelves. I had a seminar discussion with a group of young college students a few years ago. When I mentioned the Korean police action, their faces reflected the current "what?" reaction, so common today. When I questioned why they had not been taught anything about that tragic war, one of them responded; "Right now we're discussing the illegal US invasion of Iraq and Afghanistan." Viewpoints that unfortunately may be part of the ill-conceived reasoning behind some younger people seeking the exaggerated glorification of joining various terrorist organizations overseas.

What is truly upsetting, is that numerous members of this younger generation could easily become legislators, or judges or teachers in following years. Even more shocking, one of them could become president – God! – I sure hope they would do better than the previous one, and potentially, the one now in office. It's not a case of "No child left behind" anymore but rather generations of knowledge being discarded in the name of political correctness and liberal expediency. Teaching and practical applications of performing and visual arts, have been early victims of the budgetary guillotine. Sadly, too many of our youths receive most of their artistic enlightenment through the earbuds to their "iPods". That or watching exaggerated videos, featuring undecipherable lyrics or multi crotch grabbing dance routines, many more suited for advertisements touting the newest anti jock itch remedy. Not to forget the excessively violent war game videos where virtual death is exploited and mayhem the main course. Music, dance, all the performing and physical arts have become page notes in many past reports of scholastic involvement.

Very evident has been the rise of youthful defiance against any type of authority including parents, teachers and authorized agents of the government, policemen, fireman and administrators. When I was young – here he goes again - the more progressive – ultra leftist millennials will say – talking about a time too far past. But I continue.

During my youth there was the holy trinity of organization that controlled our upbringing. God, the parent and the teacher. Today the multitude of modern gods vary from cult like tent preachers to garish, TV's embellished spewing of more semantic garbage than a politician suffering verbal diarrhea. The media has exaggerated and liberal leftists politically support freedom by the younger generation, far before their adult eligibility. It has caused increased resistance against authority to either ennoble themselves to their peers or to become the major element of the next cell phone video incident going viral. Hating police has become the newest mantra for the younger generation, replacing what was once their complaint against their misinformed version of stultifying oppression by their parents. Too often distaining those who gave them birth, spent hours educating them, providing for their sustenance and sheltering them by having to, regrettably at times, go to war to protect that which allows them to continue enjoying the benefits of the freedom provided by our forefathers. Learning is the prize that requires effort and dedication to the task. It cannot be given without payment of personal time and energy to fulfill the demands placed on its acquisition.

With the inconsistent nature of parenting today, and the blasé attitude of social indecision by the millennial generation, it is difficult to distinguish fifteen-year olds from twenty-five year olds. Narcissism is being created from the devotion heaped on our latest cadre of youthful celebrities and has become a part of the youthful DNA genre.

We Digress Again – My Choice

Referred to before, I was involved in an aspect of the entertainment and special event industry during the early 1960s through the early 2000s. This allowed me, fortunately to experience some of the most popular acts of that era, and there were many. The touted "King of Pop," Michael Jackson, died at age 50. Hours upon hours of broadcast documentaries and pages of print media, were devoted to an individual, who, although very talented in his particular form of presentation, was regrettably flawed to an unimaginable degree. Accused, but cleared of highly publicized transgressions and spendthrift beyond reason, he became a poster child for the disintegration that the frantic nature of the entertainment world can produce.

An entertaining young boy with his brothers as the famed "Jackson Five", he grew in talent and performance creativity and no one can dispute his unique style and prolific imagery. We in the facility management field could count on the talented quintet to fill the house. He then retreated into a world still difficult for many of us to understand. With his death, he entered this new plastic pantheon of celebrity immortals. Still, as tragic his passing may be, many other legitimate members of the entertainment field have left us in the more recent past, a loss to both fans and the art form they popularized. "Elvis has left the building" - in a permanent sense. He was one of the modern icons of the performing field, a style never ever truly duplicated but which will be long remembered.

The major issues seeming to bring forth the greatest amount of diverse commentary and strongly held opinion in recent years are gay rights, same sex marriage and the transformation of the transgender designation to an elevated social and legal status. All this coupled with myriad of other controversies and public debates never far behind. In a quick reference, once more, regarding the immigration wrangling, one brief historical note, if you would permit.

May 13, 1939, the German transatlantic liner, SS St. Louis, sailed from Hamburg, Germany with 937 passengers, almost all Jews. After being denied entry to Cuba, their original destination, they eventually sailed on to the United States. Although faced by international and wide spread interest in this country, the Roosevelt administration's State Department refused access. Stating they had to "wait their turn on the list", based on the quota act passed in 1924. Roosevelt was reportedly contacted personally, but refused to respond. Of the over 900 Jewish passengers, a relatively small number were accepted by Britain. They survived the Holocaust, then in full surge. The remainder returned to Germany, and while some were able to find other escape routes, many were unable to avoid the "Final "Solution."

Yet today the left leaning element of politics has loudly declared their demands for uninhibited immigration. However, I believe the record indicates the Democratic Party controlled both the White House and Congress in 1939 when the St. Louis attempted to dock at our shores. I gather our then incumbent members of Congress or the Executive Branch, were too far away to feel the heat of the ovens at Dachau and Auschwitz.

As for the same-sex marriage proposition, I personally believe marriage, as has been traditionally an agreement between a man and a woman. However, so as to keep the rainbow flag carriers from bellicose demonstrations at my doorstep, I, like many citizens, will need to accept the final legal interpretation by the nine brethren and sisters in the black robes at 1 First Street, Washington, DC. For those still preparing their applications for entry to Harvard or Princeton or Columbia, that's the address of the United States Supreme Court.

I grant these congruent gender couples the equality to do as they please in the contractual or connubial relationship they have chosen. But the grotesque parades, prancing, panty wearers and attempted bizarre actions to please their liberal followers, enough is enough. Just march and wave all your flags and banners, but keep all the hugging and kissing and humping at home – please. I'm really not sure those antics are that appropriate for viewing by the kiddies brought along by all those millennial matrons who must think such outrageous performances are well suited to the Disney and Sponge Bob crowd. Again, a simple caveat. All the bearers of the rainbow flags, you should have all the rights of any citizen, just don't demand or insist on rights or benefits I am not eligible for or am refused the ability to obtain. Don't try to rain on my parade if you object to what I believe, and I won't clutter up the crowd in viewing yours.

The "gay person", is to me, ostensibly one who feels they have sensed in himself or herself, a sexual orientation that happens to be in variance to which many traditionally ascribe. And along with other attributes of our free society, that is their right to live the life they wish to pursue and not be denied those same privileges bestowed on all. Unless they purposefully perform in a manner that ultimately brings embarrassment and/or indignation by the non-gay segment, the homosexual lifestyle has been, and is, an integral part of our society. In the matter of transgender identification and recognition, for those dealing with such qualms and indecision, I can only wish them well in whatever pursuit is their choosing.

However, if the Bruce Jenner's of the world, ergo, the newly introduced Caitlin Jenner, want to wear a dress and select a more complimenting cosmetic overhaul, that's their choice. Me, I'll stick to khakis and sports shirt. Very simply, if you are an ugly or at best homely guy, you will have that same problem when you begin to shop in the ladies section of the local department store. As for becoming an attractive female, first guys, you need to have the sculptured lines that mark the normal lines of female beauty, and learn to walk in a feminine standard. Please don't prance.

However, one other mournful plea to the print and electronic media. Enough of the Kardashians. Their tasteless exploits and talentless and over exposed bodies are more suited as poster art at the "Bunny Ranch" near Las Vegas. As for the recently promoted status of the transgender, transvestite or multi sexual human configuration, very succinctly stated, I don't want to worry that my grandchildren might be forced to use restroom facilities where the opposite gender also abides. The demand to pee wherever they wish is less the right of the emotionally convoluted than the predisposition to seek voyeurism through liberalized laws.

Notable psychologists, physicians and even those who have undergone genitalia transformation – for all those Harvard experts, that's the physiological tools either gender has to work with - to move from one gender to the other has raised recent concerns of the actual emotional trauma such change can engender. The sex of a person is a biological reality. The newest demand for gender definition is, to some supposed experts, merely a misinterpretation of that reality. But then, I've always cared for my family's security and benefit and not the irrationality of the ultra-ambivalent social activists, so I leave any further discussion on that topic up to others.

Recent contentions by a few synthetic nose counters, *pollsters,* have now declared, instead of the professionally estimated two to four percent of the population being homosexual, the figure is near twenty percent. And if we were not already pummeled with polls, another plastic façade of public information, that tout more bizarre trends or concepts than the human mind can comprehend with reasonable acuity. Thus, there should be no dispute regarding same-sex marriage – right? But who cares? I know I'm at the age where there isn't enough time left to work up a sweat on any subject other than what's for my next dinner. The individual has the right to pursue his or her particular lifestyle. I stand by that freedom – it's that personal freedom I've been bellowing about in this book.

As for the sexual orientation of certain wannabe entertainment celebrities, that should be none of my business. Regrettably the gay community is forced to bear the ridiculous imagery foisted on them by a few so-called gay personalities who grossly exaggerate homosexuality with indecorous mannerisms. Among them, earlier supposed entertainer "Boy George", the prancing, swishing eunuch of exercise, Richard Simmons, and the darling of the TV fashion shows, Stephen Cojocaru(sic), that means I've found several spellings of his ridiculous appellation, not that I disagree he might be sick. Designated Hollywood's "sassy fashion critic," he enhances his dubious image with displays of exaggerated pronouncements of the latest celebrity craze. This injures the serious intent of those who just want to be themselves within a society, where they still at times, have to face undeserved scorn or rejection. The gay community has the right to be what they want to be, without harassment and bigotry, but which is too often exaggerated in the minds of their critics by the embarrassing antics of these few freaks I have just mentioned...

While still in the neighborhood of the current television menu offered a doting public – how about all those award shows. Seemingly every week, a new awards presentation. Soon they'll run out of appropriate titles and have to find other opportunities to honor some sham activity. Perhaps child molester of the month, or DUI arrest of the day. Stop with the endless presentation of statuettes and miscellaneous objects that merely indicate the recipient too often accomplished something of little value and even less importance. To list the current top ten worst TV offerings at the time of this writing would be to attempt to sow seeds in the wind. They will pass, only to be immediately replaced by equally offensive and inane presentations – kind of a lot like gall or kidney stones.

With the constant intrusion into private lives and thoughts by electronic wizardry, we are no long allowed our individual privacy. We must understand we are allowing others, often strangers, into our inner thoughts and contemplations, we relinquish a decision only we should control. The broadly accessible "You Tube" has eclipsed the TV news camera as the recording of any activity, anytime and anywhere – instantaneously and indiscriminately. "Tweeting" and "Instagram" and the addictive "Facebook" have become similar to leaving your door unlocked, the light left off and the posted announcement – *come on in – the place is yours.*

Many of we older generation remember those we considered the greats in the entertainment industry. Gary Cooper, Jimmy Stewart, Richard Burton and Marlon Brando. There was Paul Newman and the incomparable Astaire's and Gene Kelly. We still enjoy the superb performances of the iconic Clint Eastwood, Robert Redford, Sidney Portier, Al Pacino, Robert DeNiro, Morgan Freeman and so many more. Time and space preclude listing other great performers in celluloid adventures, and more recently TV movies that gave us inspiration during our supposed mundane lives. We cannot omit the women in the entertainment industry, whose talent and evocative beauty, emblazoned on numerous posters and adorned many a military locker. We enjoyed the skill and film magic of the Katherine Hepburn's, Doris Day, Claudette Colbert, and Lana Turner and of course other beauties like Betty Grable and Marilyn Monroe. The list was seemingly endless in those days, but like all things great and good and loved, they too have passed from our lives.

Let us never forget those, who during the now distant past, brought us relief from our daily troubles and the difficulties our nation faced. The comedians, the comics, those funny people, whose wit and humorous dialogue made us laugh. A laughter that was medicinally stronger than any new drug designed to offset our current doldrums or depression.

There was the hilarious George Burns and Gracie Allen, Ed Wynn and "Uncle Miltie" Berle. We can't forget the "Great One", Jackie Gleason, the inimitable Red Skelton, the hilarious Dane, Victor Borge, the frantic Lucille Ball and the irrepressible Rodney Dangerfield – who like so many of us may feel – "can't get any respect." George Carlin and Nipsy Russell, often veered ever so slightly over the line – but they were still comic giants. And Jack Benny, whose deadpan stare would convulse audiences everywhere. I must include my favorite hero of humor, Bob Hope. He was the performer for whom many in our military during past conflicts, still "thank him for the memories." I was privileged to meet a few of these individuals and host performances by a number of them in one or more of the facilities I managed. Experiencing these comedic greats, allowed my life to be enthused by such associations and gave me memories, never lost and forever cherished.

These were performers who never forgot that public obscenity, vindictive inference or the purposeful, slur was not part of true humor. However it has become the script of numerous supposed comedians and late night TV talk show hosts, whose bias and verbal onslaughts in the name of humor, too often disparage and disrespect subjects not present or available for a response or retort. We have moved politics from the serious forum to the entertainment arena. The earlier purveyors of comedic routines and dialogue were innovators and dispensers of a much needed emotional release during serious and dreadfully depressing times. The poked fun at our political and other celebrity figures. Don in a manner that brought laughter even to the faces of those the point of the humorous riposte. Lamentable as it is in this new age of free speech, a markedly increasing number of celebrity humorists have dipped their comic dialogue into the sewer of totally reprehensible output. But then again, no one ever accused them of being intellectuals and they will continually hoist the banner of First Amendment rights, having never learned or cared who fought and died to provide them that Constitutional armor.

The music we enjoyed during that era is so much different than the musical mishmash too often burdening the radio and TV programming today. There were the greats like Perry Como, Johnny Mathis, Tony Bennet, and Mr. "Blue Eyes" himself, Frank Sinatra, and so on. We can never forget the female contingent, Patti Page, Dionne Warwick, Debbie Reynolds and Rosemary Clooney, who represent just a minutia of the extensive roll of treasured ladies of song. I miss the trios and quartets and the other musical groups that produced those memorable harmonies we could whistle and hum, long after hearing them or seeing them perform.

Notwithstanding, let us pause here for a moment. This is not to disparage all the present music industry. There are many great singers and performers today, a myriad of melodies and songs that deserve, along with their performers, to become part of music history. All those past entertainment greats were probably flawed in their personal lives at times. None were perfect in the literal mode. But they also were not constantly displaying publicly questionable behavior, much as our current coterie of celebrity wannabes is prone to do, just to grace the tabloid pages. It's been said that the only difference between a star and anonymity, is success.

I was given the unique opportunity to view a passing parade of many of the latter 20th Century's finest artists, celebrities and sports icons, both personally and in performance. During my stay on this planet, I've seen the end to legally countenanced segregation and the social and economic rise of the African American community. But it is a group still on the cusp of truly experiencing their rightful place in the American society. Included, a greater and more rational acceptance of the gay community. We elected our first black – or mixed race, if that is your description – President. He had declared constantly that change will be his hallmark. To change what is ill conceived and even more invidious in its implementation, is my version of change. To demand accountability and removal of the years of bureaucratic seclusion from review, is my idea of change. Unfortunately he failed to accomplish many of those declared objectives.

Some Second or Third Thoughts – Again

The mass killing of thousands of innocents continues in many of the less endowed countries. As a deprived public, too often they are foisted on by increasing dominance of emerging warlords and depraved governments. They are ruling governments that our own national administrations' have too often supported financially over the years. And with these ongoing genocides, the response from the United Nations is one of geography. Those unaffected demur. Those, with like proclivity for trampling on the rights of their constituencies, declare ignorance that any such barbarity would ever happen within their jurisdiction. Or more often, merely exercise their veto power.

Today's hip mantra is the environment and cries for a "green culture." The latest demand is for a reduction in the gaseous diffusion created by various transportation systems and the coal industry. A few benighted sources from academia have actually blamed cattle flatulence. Based on the lack of truly substantive and legislation produced in Washington, possibly certain changes in the legislative chambers could markedly help reduce all that claimed gaseous diffusion. There are undoubtedly other methods to help reduce pollution and produce the same or greater economic output, but that is years and technological years away and I still have difficulty changing the filter on my furnace at home.

Former Vice President, Al Gore, garnered his way to a fiscal fortune and disgustingly politicized Nobel Prize on the back of the theory that global warming is occurring at an increasing pace. And worst of all, his devotees contend, the productive and technologically proficient countries alone, are causing this coming catastrophe. I suppose that leaves out Beijing, China where midday is darker than early evening in other less developed economic giants? Again, I don't have the scientific background or the mass of data to determine if what Gore, and his environmental enfant' terribles', keep proclaiming is true. Yet, parts of our nation have experienced in recent years, devastating and economically debilitating winter storms and massive expenditures by cities to keep the most basic of services operating. Then again, I suppose the brutal cold and blizzards could merely be mass hallucination. Perhaps just an aging Mother Nature having hot flashes.

Adding a note to his somewhat inconclusive resume, Mr. Gore also sold his, once personally vaunted, TV cable outlet to Al Jazeera, supposedly another of the world wide broadcasting outlets – more recently an electronic propaganda vehicle for radical Islamism. I don't doubt the sincerity of all the "green clamorers," and I agree we need to better our environment for both health and economic advantage. Yet, regardless of the merit and the support of those seeking political gain, it will take longer than tomorrow and perhaps a fair bit beyond. I don't have any of the answers and my time is far too short to add substantively to the efforts in place.

I saw tobacco finally cited for its medically harmful content, now to be replaced by the new electronic cigarette, still utilizing a substance long heralded as cancer forming. It's supposed nicotine reducing ability being heavily marketed toward the vulnerable younger generation. Illegal drug trafficking, controlled by global cartels, has expanded beyond any estimates developed years ago. The competing drug dealers have created an aura of terror and bloodshed that has far exceeded the gang warfare of the past Prohibition era. And now, supported by mealy mouthed legislative wimps, both the legalization of `pot` and its medicinal equivalents, has become the newest escutcheon of liberal freedom. Furthermore, lawfully permitted Marijuana dispensing stores and local "grass" or "weed" producing farms have emerged. The former, illegal, heretofore underground harvester and distributor of the magic plants, may have to find another line of work. I believe unemployment offices are still open. Ain't capitalism great?

Marijuana has become the recreational outlet for most of the younger generation and their *cooler and hip* elders. It has been determined when used in specific instances in particularly designed manner, it can provide certain medical benefits. But medicine aside, when a state like Colorado, California and an increasing number of other locations saw the greater benefit of increased tax revenues, I assume they have accepted the mystical invocation of now deceased drug Guru, Dr. Timothy Leary – "Turn on, tune in, drop out."

We seem to lack that populist movement that exemplified early American politics, unable to mount sufficient outrage at perceived injustices and inadequacy of representation. Bertrand de Jouvenal, French philosopher and political economist, wrote a few years ago, "A society of sheep must eventually beget a government of wolves."

As the reader will note, I've spoken little of the many people that have populated my career - my life over the years. They were special. Their faces have begun to dim for me and soon – perhaps too soon – they will have vanished completely from my sentient recollection. This I will regret, as their images have occupied and freshened my memories so often.

You will also note I have totally abstained from entering the subject of pro-life or pro-rights of the pregnant woman in this volume. Very simply, I don't feel at my age and gender that it should be my position to voice an opinion. The question of abortion and the sensitivity of the subject is for others to argue, as it is not my right to dictate any social or ethical action to any fellow human being.

Michael Moore, the porcine sized mouther of the indistinguishable, has declared, as the result of the earlier difficult Baltimore, MD police incident that all guns should be taken from police. That enough privately owned weapons would suffice and thus protect the inadvertent criminal from occasional law enforcement misconduct. Welcome to the days of Wyatt Earp and the OK Corral shootout, Mr. Moore. By the way, I understand there's a sale on at my neighborhood gun shop – bullet proof vests.

Here's a subject I've long pondered as to whether worth comment or even storing away in some dusty, little trod mental library – tattoos. What is the urge by man – and regrettably, a number of well-endowed and beauteous other gender – to cover their body in garish, meaningless, sometimes crude and often cryptic examples of what the addle-brained consider art? Of course the returning veteran often has had his or her unit insignia or service branch embellished on a visible part of his or her anatomy. Some type mark of acceptance, maturity, or inability to control ones alcohol consumption.

Or, perhaps "mother" or the name of a girlfriend left behind. Only to wish there was some effective and painless method for removing it since the named lass is long gone and the current "mon amour" is not happy with the constant reminder. But the massive array of inked doodling on arms, backs, chests and other less visible areas of the body, creates a walking version of graffiti scrawled tunnel walls, certain urban ghettos and the ubiquitous men's room at the local bus station.

Equally confusing to an aging nerd like me, the many tattoos on African-American sports figures and celebrities. Not only difficult to read, but, depending on the nature of the individual's natural color, almost impossible without microscopic inspection or possibly ultra-violet lighting. Of course such brazen expression of intellectual insufficiency is common in the prison population, who depend primarily on fellow incarcerated design incompetents to inject them with doubtful substances, via potentially infected pens. Knowing the proclivity of the ACLU to support inane projects for the sake of publicity and fund raising, they may eventually campaign to force correction institutions to employ skilled and professionally licensed tattoo providers to provide a more pleasing accompaniment to the client's 15 to 25 year sentence for a brutal crime.

As before, I just stood at the back of the crowd waiting for the parade to pass and wondering when the heroes of our youthful memories would appear to rescue us. I've long accepted the rule of unintended consequences since many of the results of my actions or of others, were normally unexpected. I don't have enough time left to be bitter or bemoan any of the less pleasant incidents in my life. Each morning's awakening informs me I'm fortunately ready for another day.

The subject of UFOs has enchanted the imagination of thousands of extraterrestrial addicts and volumes of compositions embedded with a myriad of assumptions and pure wild hypothesis. Again, I don't know if life of any sustainable form exists elsewhere. However, might I just offer a quick observation to any of those possible intergalactic visitors, were they to visit us in the future? Just be careful of the traffic – the freeways in Los Angeles are brutal. Do not consider Hollywood or San Francisco as criterion for the rest of mankind. And definitely, don't walk alone in some of our neighborhoods – particularly Southside Chicago or Detroit.

Then of course there is the verbal conflict and gastric irritation regarding the stem cell research controversy which I little understand and am at an age where its potential value would be lost on my dissipating physique. The growing dearth of water in many draught plagued areas of the southwest will continue as long as the booming population requires it as well as the desire for home owned swimming pools. The baggy, butt displaying shorts of many of our younger generational misfits, are not vexing enough to cause needless worry and self-induced insomnia. The lower their waistbands the equal designation of their minimal IQ.

One constant has followed me over my lifetime. A sincere belief that with a will and a sense of purpose, we will prevail as a nation. I've had a good life. There were many exciting moments and wonderful happenings that I was privileged to be a part of, coupled with those few difficult times. But now, nearing an eventual terminus, I can dwell on those happier, exhilarating experiences, perhaps one of the quintessential benefits of getting older.

Still in place are those groups, bent on either destruction of our present form of government, or determination to change to system to their own liking. Not only foreign despots or allied terrorist factions or those mentally misaligned home grown jihadists. There are groups here in our own country calling themselves white supremacists or Aryan protectors or pseudo citizen militias. They hide from sight like the rats in fetid sewers, and whose membership is comprised of the ill of mind. Yet, we must protect and defend their constitutional rights for their version of free expression. Which is fine so long as I can remember where the ammunition is for my shotgun.

Badly Served by So Many

We have been served badly by numerous past officialdom. The spineless Jimmy Carter, who allowed the creation of the Islamic terrorist movement, throwing the Shah under the bus and bringing to power the arch instigator of butchery in Iran, the Ayatollah "hominy grits". I rather thought that title is far more adequate. Bill Clinton, who while diddling the intern in the White House and his wife fighting the inevitable "bimbo eruption," pushed us into a fight in Somalia, then ran as he always has from anything that might taint his self-endowed legacy. Let us not omit George W. Bush whose ineptitude in entering several Mideast conflicts will ever taint his presidency. Time has yet to tell if his legacy is to be refurbished or forever buried in historical abyss. And President Barack Hussein Obama, who, if he leaned as far left in his golf swing as he does in his socialist inclinations, he'd constantly shank the ball into the woods on his many outings and Hawaiian vacations. This country has two enemies: those outside our borders who want to destroy us and those inside the Washington "beltway," who are attempting to do it from within."

The current hodgepodge of tax claims, to lower, to increase and when and to whom, has become the gist of endless political chatter. I had enough difficulty understanding the convoluted version of each new tax rule when completing my own personal return. The voluminous verbiage produced each year to supposedly simplify the current tax code, continues its tradition of confusing and not correcting past miscues. Tax filing instructions seem each year, to be as confusing as the graffiti taken from the walls of the local bus station restroom. Or perhaps, the ramblings of several monkeys, provided several typewriters and expected to eventually write the great American novel. If these increased tax codes could be printed on lighter, fluffier tissue, I'd know where to use them – my bathroom.

Another agitation to the honest taxpayer was the revelation, several years ago, of suspect examination by the IRS of applications by numerous for profit organization strictly based on their conservative origin and political affiliation. It was a dagger into the very heart of the right of the citizen in such matters. To the former President, Mr. Obama, this was done on your watch – overseen by your appointees. Any comment – worse still – why no action to correct this politically inspired invasion of personal rights?

For others having less interest in national or international buzzes of the moment, there is the concern when that "big one," the potential earthquake will strike the west coast. If it were large enough to separate California from the mainland, it could possibly float down to Columbia. Now that would serve the cartels down there more problems than they could ever imagine – higher taxes, a new very protest oriented, and excessively liberal population. Not to mention all those Hollywood celebrities, including Sean Penn, Jane Fonda and the entire staff of the Church of Scientology, plus the former Nevada casino pawn, former Senator Harry Reid, and of course the insouciant, hippy poster child, at this writing, Governor Jerry Brown. The government there thinks they have problems now with all those drug barons, just wait if California ever came floating by.

Of course there's the continual explosion of media attention every time one of the numerous consumer electronics corporations announce the newest, fastest, thinnest or application ridden cell phone update – usually only three months or less after their previous, almost identical model, had already sold millions. Tech hip fans crowd company outlets, waiting at the door for days to pay additional monies for something that beggar's description as to how it is different from its most recent predecessor. At least it reveals why most of these fad frenetic fans are not part of a list of past high school valedictorians.

And as to the tragedies brought upon the innocents by the later determined mentally maladjusted or formerly abused or safe from punishment by the legalistically twisted absence of "mens rea." A legal term used by the more liberal "bleeding hearts" to say the individual lacked the understanding of what he or she did or was not knowingly or grossly or recklessly intended. You acquire one or more automatic weapons, plenty of ammunition, plan your vicious escapade well in advance and some defense attorney, or one of those guys in the traditional long white lab coat will say, "The shooter wasn't competent at the time and thus can't be charged." Off to a nice clean, stress free stay at some mental care facility, the proverbial three hots' and a cot. That is until those guys in identical long white lab coats say all is well – "Hosanna! The person is now sane and can once more wander out into an unsuspecting public." So long as he ca remember where the nearest gun store or back alley weapons supplier is located.

I am well aware this might seem unduly harsh on those truly suffering serious mental disability. However, if the act was planned, carried out methodically or had specific targets, please have all those white coats step aside and let's investigate such horrific acts more within the guidelines of the law and the need to continual protection of the public.

My list of such non vital considerations is finally exhausted, but, if you would bear with me one last item. Draw your attention to the sports world for a moment. That last second shot from mid-court with the clock at one second, a final drive for the goal giving the gridiron championship to a team never expected to sufficiently succeed, that magic last inning, last out home run by the heretofore little known player – constantly cast as miracles. If all those happenings actually count as miracles, perhaps the Vatican has been looking in the wrong place for sainthood candidates.

Nowhere else on this conflict ridden globe can one feel they have the right to demand, and with the support of others, possibly gain a measurable voice in the conduct of their nation? I have lived in many places in the US. Additionally, also visiting a number of countries in the world while involved in projects. Places I've found, at times entertaining, but never a location I wish to spend the rest of my life. It is here in the USA I was born and will happily reside. To my listeners and readers, many of these comments herein may just seem the weakening echo of that dinosaur's roar. And like that massive creature of Jurassic movie fame, they too were dominant until overtaken by then unexpected circumstances. Much like I fear could happen to some or all of us one day.

Finally

I really don't care to attend funerals anymore. You find so many people you can't seem to remember or possibly never knew. Besides, I expect I'll be the main constituent at one myself in the not too distant future. And now, I feel more than ever it may be time to retire from the field of endeavor, time to turn over all such debates to others, better equipped and with more lifetime remaining to continue the sounding brass of disagreement.

I've written many words to be debated over your favorite beverage. If I have offended anyone's sensitivity, no one ever proved all was light and sunshine in life. I've caustically bombarded members of Congress and residents of the White House with my observations herein, surely to be condemned as unfair by all the supporters of my targets. Yet my comments were no more acrimonious than has been hurled at holders of those exalted positions since the early days of this great nation. Whomever wins future presidencies and those elected to legislative office, I fervently hope, strive to be of good will toward their constituency. But as with all matters placed in human hands, they have the discretion to be either a good, ethical, moral, sincere leader, or someone without conscience or concern for the good of the country and the people they serve. If the latter becomes fact, then we face a dire future.

My barbs aimed directly at particular portions and participants of the media, may seem excessive. But the obligation of the journalist, through whatever medium they employ, is sacrosanct in its true purpose - distribution of the truth and an honest foundation of what has happened, when, where and how. That simple formula of professionalism must be the mantra of all engaged in that activity.

To those in the entertainment field who feel I may have disavowed them of any true talent, accept the need to remember – you are the product of your media engendered celebrity. You owe your best, most skilled efforts on behalf of your audience. Not the baseless, insensitive public transgressions you seemingly feel are necessary to continue your status in the fickle and demanding entertainment and athletic world. Remember, life is an inexorable journey toward your eventual demise . . . a travel that begins immediately after your birth and cannot be halted however strong your vain belief in immortality.

When I leave this mortal domain, remaining will be the bigotry, racism, hate, hypocrisy, subterfuge, inequality, oppression of the lesser advantaged and the continual complacency by those with the power and position, to correct the list of human foibles and flaws throughout the world.

133

However, I must by the nature of the limits to individual lifetime, leave such resolution and changes to you and your progeny.

Again dear reader, remember these were my opinions, my personal viewpoints, and would in no way ever be engraved on two stone tablets such as Moses carried from the biblical mountain top. I still wonder at my age when in the not too distant future, some still undefined personality, like the movie image created by that cinema hero, John Wayne and his troop of cavalry, will sound the bugle, raise the guide on' banner, put spurs to flank and someday ride over the hill, arriving once again to vanquish the villains of our youthful imagination?

Finished – Gotcha!

About the author

James Oshust's fifty year career included executive management of major sports, entertainment and exhibition facilities; participation in management roles for the 1996 & 2002 Olympic Games, 1994 World Cup Soccer Championships and the 1998 TBS sponsored "Goodwill Games." Additionally, as an executive with one of the initial professional soccer clubs in the United States and as a consultant in facility design and operations with over forth projects domestically and abroad, including two other Olympic Games. He is the author of three novels. He, and his wife, Barbara Walsh Oshust, a former professional ice skater and recognized artist, reside in Salt Lake City, Utah.

www.ingramcontent.com/pod-product-compliance
Lightning Source LLC
Chambersburg PA
CBHW051103250726
48656CB00001B/455